CW00969563

3

£7.95
£4

# Entertainment and Ritual
## 600 to 1600

## Peter A. Bucknell

First published in 1979
by Stainer & Bell Limited
82 High Road London N2 9PW

ISBN 0 85249 444 0

All rights reserved. No part of this
publication may be reproduced, stored
in a retrieval system, or transmitted
in any form, or by any means, electronic,
mechanical, photocopying, recording or
otherwise without the prior permission
of Stainer and Bell Limited.

© Peter A. Bucknell 1979

Filmset and Reproduced by Photoprint Plates Limited,
Rayleigh, Essex.

Printed and Bound by William Clowes & Sons Limited
at Beccles and London.

# ENTERTAINMENT AND RITUAL

## 600 to 1600

by

Peter A. Bucknell

with illustrations by the author

STAINER AND BELL: LONDON

I DEDICATE THIS BOOK
to my father, my mother and my brother who
first encouraged my joy and passion for the
drama; to the scholars, writers, actors, students
and friends who have so constantly refreshed
my mind with new thoughts, information and
argument; to my dear friend Mab Goodman
for the warm hospitality of her home in Malaga
where the book was begun and finally completed, who also willingly read and discussed
the final proof; to Sheila Donaldson Walters
for her care and skill in the beautiful callig-
raphy which accompanies the illustrations;
and lastly to Allen and Rachel Percival without
whose help and enthusiasm for the book's
possibilities, my understanding of its theme
would never have been fully realised.

# Illustrations
## and
## Acknowledgements

The illustrations complement the text in dramatic terms so that the book may, in fact, be read in pictures. Nearly all the drawings are based upon material in museums and institutes, and acknowledgement is gratefully made in each case. Some, however, owe their origin to more than one source and acknowledgement is then more difficult. If, inadvertently, I have omitted to acknowledge any such source I apologise here since, as with small parts of the text, it has been hard to recall all of the words of understanding which have helped to form my judgements over a long period. In translations, I have taken the liberty of modernizing earlier English.

# Contents

# Preface

Any history, and in particular that of the performing arts, can at its best be only partially true. If an attempt be made to seek for a pattern of development there are so many gaps in extant material available (and much of this can be quite unreliable), imagination and conjecture must be exercised. Records of first known copies of plays, contemporary letters, illustrations, criticism, journals and essays, the historians, the scholars and the translators, all have to be considered in relation to the climate of their time—especially when considering the moral and political issues!

The actor or entertainer or performer (all really the same thing) has never truly been a popular figure and throughout his history, until well into this century, more often than not he was considered a vagabond, a libertine or one of the Devil's companions. He has met with abuse and has frequently been threatened with severe punishment, even with death, for his belief in his vocation.

Playhouses have been pulled down or wantonly destroyed, plays lost or adapted, or radically rewritten to serve the moral and political beliefs of the time. Methods of presentation, particularly of old plays, regularly change to suit the climate and thought of the day. Theatre means one thing today and another tomorrow. Recorders of pageants, entertainments, plays, and processions cannot always be relied upon, many wishing history to remember that their patronage or talent, money or dedication outdid everyone else. (Thirty trumpeters for a king's household is somewhat large and some 250 singing boys to accompany Saint Thomas à Becket on one of his state visits to France is large by any standards and should be considered with caution—flights of fancy in an attempt to keep up with the Joneses?)

I have tried not to take sides, but wherever possible to work from existing evidence to present this early history, and to piece together, with I hope fair conjecture, some of the gaps in information. Some early English quotations

9

and translations from Latin have been modernised for easier reading. What has fascinated me during this work is following the constant interchange of ideas through travel, intermarriage or conquest of one country by another, and to find a unified concept of thought and practice in the art of ritual and entertainment throughout most of Europe. Below the surface, traditions and practices go back far into time, mystery, and the very reason for man's existence and survival. Ideas lost with the late Renaissance emerge with the Elizabethan and some of the Jacobean playwrights, and then disappear and are not seen again until they re-emerge in Ibsen and in one or two plays which are arriving now *(Hair, Godspell, Jesus Christ Superstar?)*. Some plays and their techniques of presentation were so secret in meaning that they had to be passed on by word of mouth and not put on paper, and this also applies to music, song and dance.

I am grateful to all those writers, actors and human beings who gave me such knowledge as I have been able to retain, and hope that my personal view formed from that knowledge may add something to an understanding of this part of man's history.

*Peter A. Bucknell*
*London, August 1978*

# Introduction

With the collapse of the vast Roman Empire, Europe and its great nomadic conquerors (the Huns, Mongols, Turks, Arabs and Vikings) was a world of people on the move—migratory, invading and conquering, interchanging and exchanging their life-pattern and culture more than we care to accept or visualise. Nations were constantly on the march and intermarriage became general. The so-called Dark Ages could equally be renamed the Age of Discovery and Enlightenment, when there was a broadening and acceptance, sometimes by force or devout passion, of new spiritual and temporal beliefs.

Rome, a city in constant contact with the Near East, with the port of Alexandria which formed a permanent link with India, and with lands as far distant as China, was first invaded by the Visigoths in 410. The Visigoths and the Vandals drove through Spain and Gaul with Rome suffering its worst attack from the Vandals in 455. Then came the Huns. Along the Rhine valley the Franks (innovators of medieval culture) were already settling in 432. Young Clovis, who had made himself king of the Franks, invaded Gaul in 481 and his power ultimately extended over the northern and western areas reaching as far as the Pyrenees.

Spain was conquered by the Arabs in 711, and in 732, inspired by Mohammed, they penetrated the Western world with a great invasion on France, conquering cities and destroying churches as far as Poitiers and Bordeaux. Between 826 and 878 they invaded Crete and Sicily, attacked Rome and again established bases in the south of France, moving as far north as Burgundy. Jerusalem was captured by the Turks in 1071. Byzantium (Constantinople) was attacked from the north in 865 by the Vikings, a Germanic people living in Scandinavia. The Vikings also penetrated and invaded the Russias, Germany, Iceland, Greenland and North America. They plundered their way through France, setting fire to Paris twice, destroying on their way many of the great monasteries. Their raids extended around the Mediterranean, past Gibraltar, threatening Rome, whilst they concentrated their main invasion on England, Ireland, Scotland and northern France (Normandy). They set up a kingdom in Ireland and began to settle in England, chiefly in the north-east, slowly to take over a despotic rule of the rest of the country.

The Britons and the Celts had been invaded from Rome by Julius Caesar, but it was Claudius (41–54) who, possibly in order to protect the coast of France, began the conquest of the islands which led to the conversion of the British to much of Roman and Mediterranean custom, thought and belief. When in the middle of the fifth century the Romans finally withdrew from Britain, to protect their Empire from the barbaric invaders, Britain was defenceless and was from that time on attacked by various tribes, Teutonic in origin: the Jutes, the Angles (thus Angleland or England), the Saxons, and the Picts from the north. Some of the Britons escaped by crossing to France, becoming known as the Bretons. The Angles and the Saxons settled in the south-east of England and the Romanised Celts and Britons were slowly driven north, north-west and west to Wales, Scotland and Cornwall during the fifth and the sixth centuries.

The conquest was complete by 615 with Roman and British culture existing side by side. The practice of human sacrifice, the worship and sanctification of the oak-tree and the continued reverence of many old accepted gods was common, or went 'underground' with the conversion of the Anglo-Saxons to Christianity. Some of these gods are still preserved today in the names of the days of our week—Thursday ('Thorsday'); Wednesday ('Wodensday') etc. There was also the dread goddess Wyrd by whom man's destiny or fate was determined. In the seventeenth century she must still have exercised strong power—Shakespeare conceived her as a trinity in the 'weird' sisters who foresaw the fate of Macbeth.

By the eleventh century England was for the most part under Anglo-Saxon rule, the Vikings and Danes having been subdued and driven back to their own country by Alfred of Wessex, and it was during this century that England, Byzantine southern Italy and the Muslims of Sicily were conquered by the Normans. They were a vigorous and ambitious mixture of the Viking and the Frank. William the Bastard, Duke of Normandy by marriage, was the heir to the throne of England. He, with his knights, missionaries, abbots and bishops, brought with him to England French culture which was to dominate the English language, learning and customs for the next several hundred years.

Christianity of some kind was established in England during the second century. It is said that Glastonbury Abbey was established by Christ's first disciples. Glastonbury is associated with Saint Joseph of Arimathea and the Holy Grail is traditionally accepted as a receptacle containing some of the sweat and blood of Jesus Christ. England, like most European countries, was missionary orientated. Saint Columban invaded the Continent and took his missionary fervour to what is now called Switzerland. Saint Boniface founded many monasteries in Germany, and it was he who showed great concern that women should not join pilgrimages for fear that they should not remain pure but turn to harlotry. Religious Britain was also in contact with the Orient through Lombardy and the eastern Alps. Irish clerics even founded houses as far away as Iceland. Saint Augustine converted King Ethelbert to Christianity and in 597 established the see of Canterbury, where an old Romano-British church possibly stood on the site of the present cathedral. Many of the clergy read Greek and were specialists in the beautiful copying and decorating of the sacred texts. By the late eleventh century crusaders were marrying Armenian and other local women. Their children were brought up and educated by the people of the country. They learnt Arabic and the mystery of numbers, and the power of geometric shapes, bringing back to their homeland many of their adopted customs, including new fashions in behaviour, clothing, and a wide variety of spices, fabrics and crafts. Man was discovering many new, beautiful and precious things to influence his life. Some innovations caused criticism—a monk of Canterbury writes 'Nearly all the young men of the court grow their hair long, like girls. Then with tresses well combed, glancing about them and winking in ungodly fashion, they daily walk abroad with delicate steps and mincing gait'.

The Middle Ages saw the continuation of this fusion of many cultures. The world was mysterious and full of questions. By the end of the thirteenth century everybody was on the move: doctor, scholar, tinker, tailor, soldier, sailor, beggarman, thief. Nuns, monks and bishops headed for Rome; pilgrims—men, women and children—made for the Holy Land, where the map-makers sited Jerusalem as the centre of the world with the head of Christ to the east, toward the rising sun; knights, soldiers and mercenaries fought the Crusades all over the Near East. Everywhere they went entertainers joined or went with them.

The travelling professional entertainers originally migrated from Rome. Justinian had closed the theatres at the beginning of the sixth century, and, with constant enemy invasion, entertainers of all kinds ('variety') took to the

13

roads, journeying up into France and northern Europe. They led a nomadic life, playing on street corners and in town squares, taking to the country in small groups or even alone. They performed at weddings and big festivals, welcomed by kings and noblemen living in their dark and gloomy castles. Few employing these entertainers could read or write, and it must have been a glad and warming sight to know that a group of performers had arrived. Many gave them unconditional accommodation so that the long dark evenings and cold winters, the periods of enforced imprisonment because of weather or fear of siege from an enemy, could be made somewhat less monotonous.

Roman players were trained in a theatre which demanded speech and song, dance, mime, music and spectacle, as well as puppet shows, contortionists and acrobats (some performing naked), sword swallowers and fireeaters, 'blue-nose' comedians and dancing girls from the Near East. There were the straight story-tellers, musicians and folk singers, as well as animal trainers with their menageries. These were the forerunners of the professional entertainers of the High Middle Ages.

Travelling actors from the old Roman comedies and farces brought with them their stock characters, stage 'business' and rustic plots (forerunners of the *commedia dell'arte*) improvising and incorporating local gossip and stories of the towns and villages they visited. They used a simple platform stage and a painted backcloth (as their families had done before them) as their one and only setting—a street scene. No script survives, only the names of some of the characters in the plays. The *Saturae* ( = 'full of different things') and the *Saturnalia*, typical early forms of Roman entertainment connected with ancient wine and fertility festivals, may well also have travelled far from their country of origin.

Classical scholars migrated, moving east and north during the early years of Christianity with knowledge not only of Terence, Plautus and Seneca but also the plays of Aeschylus, Sophocles and Euripides. Hroswitha, a Benedictine abbess of Gandersheim living in Saxony in the tenth century, wrote comedies and religious plays after the model of Terence, a strange link with the mystery and morality plays which were to appear much later in the history of medieval drama. They contained characters both from the Holy Scripture and abstract, similar to characters like 'Good Deeds' and 'Fellowship' in the play *Everyman*. One early play, *The Passion of Christ*, contained several hundred lines in Greek out of Euripides' plays, including passages nowhere else preserved.

Julius Caesar, who travelled with his 'Mimes', possibly introduced them to Britain and it is equally possible that the Roman soldiers brought with them their cults derived from the worship of Serapis in Egypt. They certainly built their theatres or places of entertainment whilst occupying Britain as can be seen, for one example, at Verulam (Saint Albans). First used as areas for staged fighting, dance and mime, later architectural developments suggest that they may have been used for the production of small plays.

The migratory professional entertainer was always in trouble with the Church even though he may have influenced the style and manner of the sacred services. During the second century an elder of the Church asked whether 'the God of Truth, who hates falsehood, can receive into his kingdom those whose features and hair, age and sex, sadness and laughter, love and anger, are all pretence'.

As early as the beginning of the fourth century actors were threatened with excommunication, the Church deciding that actors supported the worship of false gods by acting in theatres of pagan origin. The professional entertainer led a difficult and dangerous existence under this threat and the knowledge of eternal damnation.

Thomas de Chabham of Salisbury wrote at the end of the thirteenth century:

There are three kinds of HISTRIONES [actors]. Some transform and transfigure their bodies in indecent dance and gesture, and without any decency unclothe themselves and wear grotesque masks. There are others who have no definite profession, but act as vagabonds, not having any permanent home; they frequent the Courts of the great and say scandalous and shameful things concerning those who are not present so as to delight the rest. There is also a third class of *Histriones* who play musical instruments for the delight of men, and of these there are two types. Some frequent drinking places and lewd gatherings, and sing their stanzas to move men to lasciviousness. There are others, who are called *Jongleurs*, who sing of the gestes [actions] of princes and the lives of the saints.

The *Jongleur* was a minstrel or professional 'minister' of entertainment who recited verse with appropriate gestures and could play a musical instrument. Petrarch likened their function, in the development of literature, to that of the book publisher. Guilds for minstrels were formed in France in 1321 but not in England until 1469. They were graded into three groups: first were the poets and musicians; the travelling actors were relegated to the second grade; and lastly came the riff-raff (fire-eaters, rope-walkers, acrobats and tumblers, conjurors, animal trainers and so on).

Not only did minstrels perform at courts, fairs and other celebrations, but they also accompanied pilgrims, telling their stories or singing their songs as a change from the pilgrims' own repertoire of chant. They alone kept alive professional traditions until the arrival of the morality plays and the interludes. Some became permanent entertainers attached to a court— the jesters. A few became rich and were licensed to perform before the great households, richly and gaudily dressed and escorted by several attendants. Most lived a miserable existence exiled by the Church in an order passed in 1281, which decreed that 'No clerks shall be Jongleurs, Goliards or Bufoons'!

The goliards were not in a sense professional but were wandering scholars and clerks of the early Middle Ages who decided to 'drop out' from conventional life and become 'hippies', joining up with the travelling actors and entertainers, originally singing Latin poetry. Some authorities suggest that the professional court jester and the amateur goliard between them produced the troubadour.

The Troubadours of the eleventh, twelfth and thirteenth centuries came from southern France (the Provençal verb *trouver* meaning 'to find' or 'to invent') and from northern France (called *trouvères*) in the twelfth, thirteenth and fourteenth centuries. These performers were the élite—one distinguished himself by becoming abbot of the Cistercian abbey of Thoronet in the south of France—and England, with its long and strong connections with the courts of France, must have received many of them. They wrote their own lyrics, usually on a passionately amorous theme. The stories they sang described their constancy and servitude to a cold and remote lady, asking her to be free with her love either platonically or, better still, in bed. In the eyes of a mistress so minded a troubadour could have, symbolically, taken the place of a husband away fighting on a crusade. Accordingly he invented a whole vocabulary of erotic signs and symbols. There are many parallels today in our folk and pop singers composing and performing their own songs and music—remote yet highly stimulating physically and emotionally to their lonely listeners!

Most troubadours had a group of followers. We can recall something of these travelling entertainers from troupes that still exist in many countries and for whom rules and restrictions still make for a hazardous and difficult life. In the south of France travelling companies regularly arrive at a small village or town in the morning, give a performance in the evening, then pack up and move on to the next town some thirty-odd kilometers away. Usually they are a group of young people or a family—father, mother, children, grandparents and the odd uncle or aunt or close friend. They carry in their cars or van all their belongings—costumes, gaudy and cheap trappings of simple scenery, properties and sound equipment, plus two or three spotlights, a couple of 'floods' and their cooking apparatus and bedding. They are groups of singers, dancers, acrobats, clowns and the odd animal trainer—all doubling up and helping one another out, performing mostly on public holidays and on saints' days. The older members of the company take money for the price of a ticket (or pass the hat around after the performance for a general collection), assist in putting up the slack wire, help with the scene changing, cook for the troupe and do all the odd jobs. The younger children are just starting off on their professional careers and always draw good applause from an often thin audience as they command dogs to jump through hoops covered with brightly coloured tissue paper, or perhaps make their début with father on a not very high trapeze, prettily dressed in pastel frilly costumes and already behaving in a very professional manner—entertainers close to the earth such as these are recorded time and time again by many painters including Picasso and Rouault. In Provence, Spain and Italy, street musicians, not beggars but wandering minstrels, may still remind us of their ancestors.

Not so very long ago in the streets of many an English town the arrival of the circus with its Grand Parade to the open-air 'showground' was still an annual attraction. At the seaside was the Punch and Judy show on the beach whilst on the promenade the brass band played in its beautifully decorated stand. Or there was the delight of the pierrot troupe or concert party or nigger minstrel show at the end of the pier. In London, there remains only the rare busker entertaining a cinema queue and the occasional flute or guitar wafting its music up the stairs from an underground station where young students make music for hours on end, depending on the odd coins for their bread and butter. Perhaps we shall need the travelling entertainer again to brighten life in the 1980s as they did only forty years or so ago when, as a child, I remember street dancers in grotesque female costume; artists decorating household plates with the black smoke from candles, revealing, as if by magic, portraits of our King and Queen and famous political personalities; paper-tearers using folded newspapers and, by cunning, transforming them into patterns like lace snowflakes or great fir-trees over eight feet tall; the escape artiste, locked and bound by chains, put into a sack and—hey presto!—within minutes emerging free of his manacles; the man with his performing dog; and the Italian with his dressed-up monkey and his barrel organ.

These artistes were not beggars; they were professionals who had entertainment in their blood. They were our heritage from their forbears—the migratory performers of Rome and the early Middle Ages.

ENTERTAINMENT & AMUSEMENT

A Man playing a Double Shawm & a Woman dancing with Bells 12th

Based on Manuscript Drawings

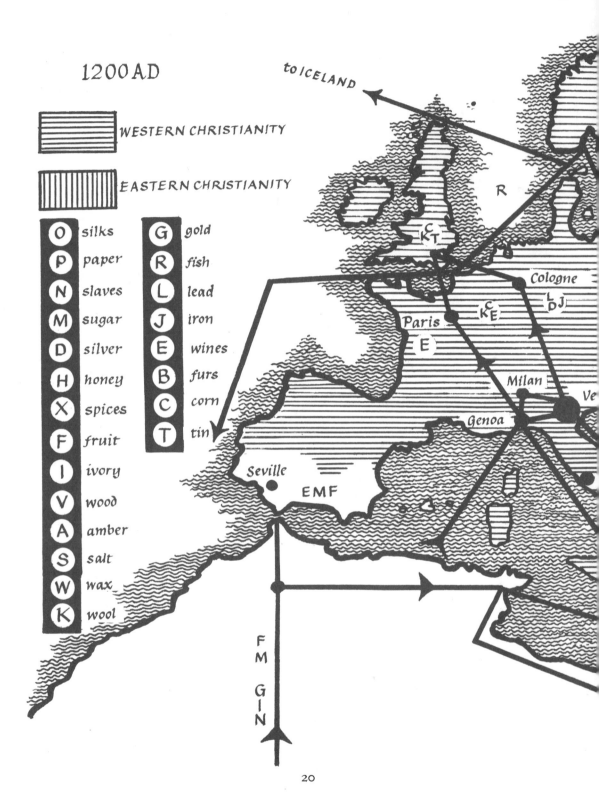

## 1200 AD

WESTERN CHRISTIANITY

EASTERN CHRISTIANITY

| | | | |
|---|---|---|---|
| O | silks | G | gold |
| P | paper | R | fish |
| N | slaves | L | lead |
| M | sugar | J | iron |
| D | silver | E | wines |
| H | honey | B | furs |
| X | spices | C | corn |
| F | fruit | T | tin |
| I | ivory | | |
| V | wood | | |
| A | amber | | |
| S | salt | | |
| W | wax | | |
| K | wool | | |

to ICELAND

R

C
K T

Cologne

L
D J

Paris

K C
E

E

Milan

Genoa

Ve

Seville

EMF

F
M
G I
N

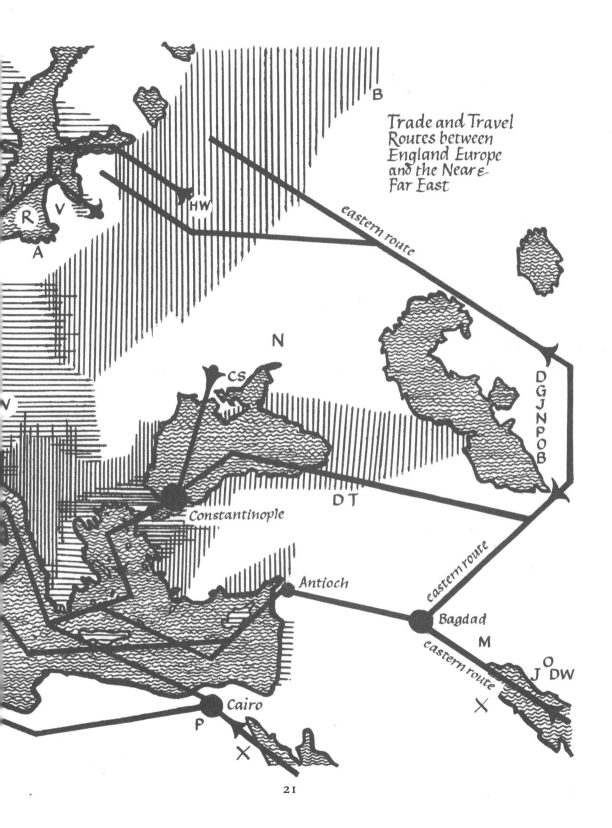

Trade and Travel
Routes between
England Europe
and the Near &
Far East

eastern route

B

HW

R V

A

V

N

CS

DGJNPOB

DT

Constantinople

Antioch

eastern route

Bagdad

M

J O DW

eastern route

Cairo

P

21

Based on Early Manuscript Drawings

12th

A Group of Travelling Entertainers

Most of these
Acts show
direct links
with Eastern
Entertainers

# Prologue

I pray you all give your audience
And hear this matter with reverence.
By figure a moral play:
The summoning of Everyman called it is,
That of our lives and ending shows
How transitory we be all day.
This matter is wondrous precious,
But the intent of it more gracious,
And sweet to bear away.
The story saith: Man, in the beginning
Look well, and take good heed to the ending,
Be ye never so gay!
Ye think sin in the beginning full sweet,
Which in the end causeth the soul to weep,
When the body lieth in clay.
Here shall you see how Fellowship and Jolity,
Both Strength, Pleasure, and Beauty,
Will fade from thee as flower in May:
For ye shall hear how our Heaven King
Calleth Everyman, to a general reckoning:
Give audience, and hear what he doth say.

*Everyman*

24

# 1

# In the Church

## The Mysteries

Man's life became centred on and dominated by the Church. The actual building was not only the place of the mysteries and of solemn worship but it was also a refuge for the weary and the sick, caring for the poor and giving beds to the ailing and the aged. In London separate hospitals were set up in churchyards to look after pilgrims on their way to the shrine of Saint Thomas à Becket—one at Southwark Cathedral. In turn, round the hospitals came the alms-houses, leper colonies and homes for orphans. The Church alone was responsible for schooling and education, and for entertainment and splendid ritual celebrations. Meetings of all kinds were held within the church walls, for in most places the church was the only large building other than the castle or the manor house. Rushes and sweet smelling herbs scattered its floors for comfort and for warmth. No important event in town or village life could pass by without some celebration there—including civic and legal meetings. It was commonly a storing house for hay and grain as well. Man wandered in and out of it as we do today in closed or open market complexes, meeting friends, gossiping about rising costs and his neighbours, the bad weather and its effect on the crops, perhaps at the same time making a deal on the price of a head of cattle or a piece of land.

We are so much accustomed now to a formal remote pattern of behaviour in church, taking part in a service only too often attended by a meagre twenty or thirty bodies, with whispered singing and chilly responses to the prayers of the clergy, that we forget that in the beginning the church had an atmosphere encompassing a large congregation of lusty communicants held together by a deep and mystical experience.

Today some of this atmosphere still remains in Europe and we can imagine from watching vignettes in parts of France, Spain, Italy, Greece or Yugoslavia what English society in the Middle Ages must have been like in and around the parish church or cathedral. In a village church in Italy four candles surrounding an open coffin on bare wooden trestles shed their light on the mortal remains of some old member of the parish whilst children play hopscotch or other simple games down the aisles. In a French cathedral two amorous young people flirt in a side chapel whilst solemn mass is celebrated in another. An obvious tourist, in clothes betraying his country of origin, buys souvenirs from the church 'shop'. In Greece, the bride and bridegroom give presents after their wedding to everyone in sight, be they friends, relations or total strangers; a fiddler waits outside, peeing against the side of the church but ready to accompany the bridal party to the local hostelry for dancing, drinking and feasting. In churches large and small, the beggars hope—sometimes asleep, sometimes sick; gypsies wait to tell a fortune; and a youth may even solicit trade for the local 'house of ill-repute'. All these I have seen happening within a church whilst the devout are at their confessional or lighting candles before Our Lady: there is no reason to suspect that life was much different in medieval England.

Some European churches also still tell us what the inside of a medieval church looked like, with their walls richly covered with amateur narrative paintings; surrounding the one or many altars, they proclaim miraculous cures and escapes from death at sea or on the land, a pictorial record for all to see and revere. In Greece, young and old still buy little tin replicas of various parts of the human body, and hang them on the walls or put them by the altar (or a particular icon) to give thanks, usually anonymous, for being restored to good health after sickness or disease. Perhaps the best (or worst) surviving example of ritual encompassing all that is good and all that is bad is to be seen at Lourdes—the belief in the divine miracle hand-in-hand with vulgar commercial enterprise. Medieval man had to come to terms with both during his life's span, just as we do.

The early Church contained the world and taught her congregation accordingly. Few in the entire populace could read or write and they certainly did not understand the Church's language, Latin. Every visual object therefore had to tell its story simply and directly. Wall paintings and pictures, stone and wood carvings, altar furniture, stained glass, the tiled floors, embroidered and woven hangings, and the vestments of the clergy all had their story to tell. Colour, symbol, proportion, motif or shape could all be read just as we immediately recognise Santa Claus by his red suit and white beard or a policeman by his dark navy blue uniform and distinctive headgear.

The Church also controlled the production of books. The cathedral is a book—a picture-book of instruction with its design in the hands of the clergy alone. The second Council of Nicaea in 787 decided that the design and composition of all religious symbol and imagery and dramatic representation, including place, scale, size, colour and arrangement within the church, should be controlled by the Church alone and not left to the caprice of the craftsmen, who should only be responsible for its execution.

Originally in the hands of clerics who were artist-craftsmen, work was soon given over to non-clerical craftsmen and peasants. Rich and poor alike worked together in the building of their church. The lords gave their land, the merchants their money, and the peasants their labour. Professional skills were supplied by the master-builder and the clerk of works, with their team of rough masons, free masons, sculptors, carvers, carpenters, glaziers, painters and metal-workers. Nuns and local women wove and embroidered the hangings and the vestments for solemn service.

This pictorial imagery revealed all that the Church thought necessary for man to know—the history of the world from its creation by God the Father, including the history of the lives of the saints and the martyrs, knowledge of the arts, crafts and sciences, dogma, and the understanding and order of the virtues and vices. Visual 'teaching aids' covered every possible surface outside and inside the building.

During the middle of the thirteenth century the Bishop of Beauvais wrote a massive book in four parts called *Speculum Majus*, recording everything that man should know. In Book 1, 'The Mirror of Instruction', he not only begins with the story of the Fall and explains the riddle of the Universe, but also writes about various branches of mundane knowledge including the mechanical arts—for by the labour of his hands man begins the work of his redemption. Book 2, 'The Mirror of History', is a history of man, his struggles, sufferings and his achievements in the battle of the soul (which in the end was for the Bishop the sum total of the world's history): it was a history of man himself watching his progress under the eyes of God. Book 3, 'The Mirror of Nature', explains the order, created by God, of natural phenomena. The days of the Creation in turn record the four elements, fishes, birds, beasts, the minerals and all vegetation and so on. Lastly there is 'The Mirror of Morals', which is very closely related to 'The Mirror of Instruction'. It states that knowledge is but a means to a virtue, for the end of life is not to know but to have *acted*. This use of the word 'acted' is not coincidental.

Almost all the average man knew of his faith was through what he could see. Ritual was visual . . . and dramatic.

Christ on the cross, in the early Church, was represented in magnificence and glory—richly dressed and crowned.

The Magi, by their appearance, represented youth, maturity and old age.

The Virgin wore a veil as a symbol of her virginity.

The font had a lid to keep out evil spirits.

The Ark represented God's House.

Man's arrival in the Kingdom of Heaven was represented by two angels emerging from clouds carrying in a basket the soul of the reclining tomb effigy below up to God, who waits sitting patiently on his throne.

The symbols of the seasons and of work were represented in the meaning of the months. Human characteristics such as cowardice, harshness, and disobedience all had their place in the scheme, as did the terrors of Hell which were continually depicted in the most violent imagery of that which would happen to the sinner—boiled, tortured, raped, buggered or shat upon for eternity by devils of similar persuasions. Monstrous creatures resembled part man, part wolf, bat, insect, pig, ass or ape— imagery as old as history. The gargoyles high up spewed from their mouths the rain and dirt collected in the gutterings.

As dramatic properties, all church furniture contained a hidden 'mystery'. Above the altar was placed a symbolic crown, a richly decorated circular band of metal or gold, set with precious stones. Seven oil lamps were attached to it as according to Revelations, IV.5, 'There were seven lamps of fire burning before the throne which are the seven spirits of God'. Sacred vessels and objects of ritual placed upon the altars were usually of gold and enriched with precious gems and stones. Everywhere lighted tapers and candles were a constant reminder of 'The Light of the World'. The Sanctus bell when rung symbolised that knowledge of the scriptures should immediately be put to 'action'. It was suspended from a frame in the shape of a cross, and the cord which rang this bell was made from three twisted threads—the three-fold interpretation of the scriptures.

Contact with daily life introduced more naturalistic imagery as opposed to the early mystical abstract symbols—which included fire, light, wax, water, oil, and incense. The adder was the image of the sinner, the lion often paired with the lamb became the symbol of peace, and the dragon represented the devil. The lectern was fashioned in the shape of Saint John's eagle with outstretched wings to support the Gospel. The dove, the fish, and the symbol of immortality—the peacock or the phoenix—all had their place. Ceilings in Roman churches all over Europe were decorated to represent a night sky full of stars to represent the heavens.

Some of the images could be made to move by mechanical means. There is one, an animated figure of Christ on the Cross (Cluny Museum, Paris) dating from the twelfth century, which contains a spring connected by an iron rod to a lever that the manipulator worked with his foot to make the head, mouth and eyes of Christ move. In the 'act' of ritual the controller may well have been a ventriloquist, to make more impact on the watchers.

Regulations formed by the interpreters of the Bible had created a pattern which, by the thirteenth century, was not particular to any one country. Images with their all-seeing eyes and the cherished relics of saints revealed a hidden inner life—objects of contemplation to move the soul. Gregory of Nyssa (335?–394) stated 'Silent paintings tell their stories from a wall'. In the sixth century Pope Gregory the Great had asked for 'the painting of figures in churches in order that the illiterate may be able to read from the walls what they are unable to read in books'. Another means of visual instruction is recorded in a manuscript illumination showing a priest chanting the 'Exultat' from a text whilst unrolling it over and down the front of his pulpit with, at intervals at the side of the text, pictures painted upside down illustrating what is being said. These narrative pictures would be seen by his listeners the right way up. The priest/narrator must surely also have dramatised his story-telling.

All that was designed, then, spoke its story. Every object contained knowledge and a mystery, and the representation was never personal, for it came from God the Father: man should never impose his will over that of his Father.

Medieval society had a passion for order and symbol. The painters—designers of the 'sets' before which ritual acts were performed—knew that lines described in concentric and twisting rhythms would be read as the sky, and a stalk with a few leaves at once became a tree. The early symbol for a city was simply a rectangle with an opening. If, however, the town had been destroyed, then the symbol was described upside down.

Sacred mathematics and proportion were equally important to the architect and craftsmen who built the settings: the church was orientated from the movement of the sun with the head of the church exactly facing East, and the East window was enriched by the most magnificent glass; the North was usually consecrated to the Old Testament and the South to the

New; the West became the region of death, the facade filled with carvings depicting Christ sitting enthroned whilst the Last Judgement enfolds below him, and the West door represented Christ himself, 'The Celestial Door'. Every door had its meaning. The ground plan of the church was the image of Christ crucified, his head the chancel surrounded by the chapels of the saints, his heart the principal altar, and the doors his hands and feet. The spire 'aspired' heavenwards.

The 'properties' used in Christian ritual were also well-known symbols. The orb, carried by the Lord, represented the world from which the cross ascends as a symbol of enlightenment. The sceptre ('I rule') became one of the symbols of kings and emperors. The Greek 'P' (pi) became a simplified hooked staff, or shepherd's crook, and stood for the pastoral responsibility of a bishop. Symbols or signs of the Zodiac, from the thirteenth century on, also made their appearance in church design, influenced by the Crusades and contact with the divided Churches of Rome and Byzantium. Saint Thomas Aquinas established a concept of the Creation based on a combination of Aristotelian logic and Christian mystery—a great living step-ladder between heaven and earth with everything in its rightful place—and at the centre was man, the image of God. High above lived the angelic beings who governed the stars, the moon, the sun and the planets, which in turn ruled the elements, animals, plants, stones, and man. Everything therefore was affected from above and below. The signs of the Zodiac thus were related to the various parts of man's body. Man became a composite of the twelve signs and was governed by the planets which in turn determined the code of colours in heraldry and their relation to jewels and to stones.

| Planet | Stone | Heraldic Tincture | |
|--------|-------|-------------------|--|
| Sun | Topaz | Or | (Gold) |
| Moon | Pearl or Crystal | Argent | (Silver) |
| Venus | Emerald | Vert | (Green) |
| Mercury | Amethyst | Purpure | (Purple) |
| Jupiter | Sapphire | Azure | (Blue) |
| Mars | Ruby | Gules | (Red) |
| Saturn | Diamond | Sable | (Black) |

Those who could afford to employ their own astrologers did so and many a moment of decision involving politics, the building of a city, the conception of a child or the diagnosis of sickness was determined by the position of the stars and the planets, with the moon always affecting a moment of crisis.

Europe was busily at work building great churches and cathedrals and in all of them (including York, Canterbury, Wells and Ely) the interior and the exterior of the buildings were made brilliant with bright colours. Images and ornament, of stone and wood, in weaving and embroidery, in glass and paintings on the walls, were more often than not represented in full colour. Medieval man, approaching and entering one of his great churches, was faced and then surrounded by all the colours of the rainbow.

Sometimes God's house was shared by a saint, buried there, and became a place of regular pilgrimage. The nave then grew longer and extra passages were formed for great processions and to direct the faithful towards the high altar, the tomb and the relics of the saint. Special chapels, set around the apse and in the crypt, were prepared for the mortal remains or holy relics (pieces of bone, blood, wood or cloth) brought to the church from often far distant lands. The relics could be seen through glass panels set in golden images or caskets, or were hidden by a concealed door, only displayed at special times when many would make solemn pilgrimage (followed by a festival of dancing, singing, and, in many cases, drinking).

Dance and song were part of man's means of self-expression. In early Christian times the bishop led the dance in the choir of the church. It was also believed that, during the solemn service, the angels were present with Christ in the choir, singing and dancing in the celebration of the Divine Mystery. But it was always getting out of hand. A decree in the eighth century forbade 'dancing places' in and about the church. The history of dance in church is best found in Spain, mainly because of the complaints recorded. But since many pilgrims made their way to shrines such as Compostela it is highly likely that priests everywhere faced difficulties in deciding how far to allow 'pagan' dancing to enter their churches. It may also be that Spanish clergy were particularly sensitive . . . since nothing could be more solemn than the national dance of Spain, the pavan. More likely, as the complaints were made mostly in the south of Spain, the priests (and their Pope in Italy) were afraid of Moorish, Muslim influence entering their Church with 'lascivious' gesture in the normal dance.

In the twelfth century the Pope ordered that there should be no dancing within the church save for the *seises* (young choristers permitted to dress up and dance on special feast days before the altar). Seises were allowed to continue with their dancing, it is said, until their dresses fell to pieces. Many churches, to evade this ruling, cut the existing dresses into small

31

sections and appliquéd one piece to each new dress, thus allowing the custom to continue. This sacred dance is still performed, thanks to a special bull of Eugenius IV which was authorised in 1439, in Seville Cathedral where the choristers dance in the space between the choir and the high altar accompanied by the sound of the castanets. At the shrine of the Virgin of Montserrat pilgrims, during their vigils, danced and sang, and it was still the custom to dance before the sacred images in the churches of Toledo, Jerez, Seville and Valencia during the time of Saint Thomas of Villanueva, bishop of Valencia. Dancing in fact was encouraged. In Catalonia and Roussillon, the most Spanish of the French provinces, religious dancing continued well into the seventeenth century. Gitanos regularly danced with their tambourines and sang before the shrines and sacred images. Pre-Christian dance and customs existed side by side with Christian doctrine. An account of a pilgrimage today may help us to understand what it must have been like to go to, say, Compostela from Canterbury.

For several days we had been riding on very bad roads, more like mud tracks, to visit a remote basilika to see some of the several hundred frescoes there. Several times on our slow journey we passed men, women and children, many of the groups obviously forming complete families. There were parties, too, of more than twenty. Some were travelling in open carts, others on horse and many were just walking, but all going in our direction. Their costumes varied as did their faces, indicating that they came from different parts of the country and perhaps even further. Some we recognised as Muslims, with the women veiled and in baggy trousers; others dressed in old grey suits; others were in costume tightly bound with strips of richly coloured embroidery.

On our arrival at the basilika, which was small, not measuring much more than 100 feet either way, we met many of our fellow travellers again—they had all been converging on our destination, the church. Rough open-fronted long huts of wood had been built on either side of the precincts surrounding the basilika, from east to west. Young lads and children had been gathering fern and bracken which was to provide comfortable sleeping areas for the men and women. Areas had also been provided for washing and cooking. All was very simple.

On entering the church, in the central area, hardly more than fifty feet square, a solemn service was being conducted by priests whom we recognised by their dress to be members of the Orthodox faith. The thousands of figures in the paintings were beautifully preserved, other than that all the eyes were defaced with a cross, probably made by the point of a sword. This told us that at one or more times the basilika had been conquered by Muslims and converted into a Mosque. The obliteration of the vision of the figures meant that they had lost their mystical powers. This and the change of the position of the place of prayer, now pointing to Mecca, were the only alterations made by the invaders—how civilised compared to what the maniacs of the Reformation and the Puritans did to stamp their belief on English churches!

We had arrived on a very special day. Today, we were told, the patron saint had been taken from his place of rest, robed and crowned and displayed—a ceremony occurring perhaps only once in a lifetime. The priests, seemingly oblivious of the constant coming and going of our friends, the pilgrims, continued with their service. We were onlookers bewildered by what we saw. Most were involved with their own rituals and mystical ceremonies. One very old lady continually walked around a stone tomb, kneeling at each corner, making the sign of the cross. This was repeated for the entire length of time we remained in the basilika— some two or more hours. A mother, accompanied by her little boy, placed and rubbed her hands on a piece of carved stone and repeatedly returned to her child where she then played her hands on his face, making a continuous gesture as if washing the forehead and cheeks. Was this some ancient cure for a skin infection or disease of the head? A shabbily dressed man, walking around the perimeter of the church, held a lighted candle in front of him and another behind, moving them to make the symbol of the cross. Tiny amounts of money were left everywhere . . . on corners of tombs, ledges and on the floor.

Outside the church people were singing, some dancing, others busily engaged preparing food. The festival looked as if it might continue for several days. More were still arriving on our departure, more perhaps were still to come from their villages and smallholdings to take part in an important ceremony in the calendar or their lives—the precious reappearance of their beloved saint.

This account is only twelve years old, from a visit to the province of Montenegro in Yugoslavia. We had entered a world and an act of belief which must have been very similar to the early foundations of the Christian Church. Orthodox ritual and dogma gave place and space to personal ritual and belief—if to our eyes somewhat 'pagan' (whatever that word means any more). The priests were encompassing in the formal and solemn service the deep and individual expression of the visitors. Each respected each. Each had one supreme common denominator: God!

Christian liturgy, like all other forms of medieval art, is a constant chain of order, form and pattern in its symbolism. The structure of the solemn mass with its use of speech and sound, movement and gesture, the dress worn, the colours used and the altar furnishings is the first form of drama to be found in England which is specifically recorded and written down.

It includes carefully stated direction to those taking part, the celebrant assisted by the deacon or sub-deacon, the choir and the acolytes or servers. Between 800 and 900, elements elaborating the mystical dramatic re-enactment of the Last Supper were being added. Pagan or pre-Christian festivals began to reappear like Christmas and Harvest Thanksgiving—and in particular the great Easter celebrations. The earliest sacred 'services' (that is, the serving of communion) were held in catacombs and cemeteries, but later in private houses. Great was the punishment to those discovered taking part. When the mass was allowed to be taken freely without fear of persecution the building for its celebration was based *in memoriam* on a Roman temple or senate-house, rectangular in shape with a semi-circular niche at one end facing east, where originally the Roman consul would sit with his advisors to pass judgement on some person who had broken the law or was seeking advice. Early Christian priests replaced the throne with a table (altar) and here was the beginning of the pattern of positioning in relation to the celebration of the mass.

Instruction and participation were on three levels. Because of the language barrier the visual elements of mime, movement, costume, colour, and furniture were very important. The newcomers understood a simple story or narrative. Those who had participated for some time grew to read the meaning beyond the symbol whilst the fully initiated discovered a personal divine truth.

High feast days produced the most complicated and spectacular directions for processions and 're-enactments' prior to and during the performance of the mass. Easter week became the central event—during the celebration of the Paschal Mystery (concerning the passing from slavery to freedom), 'We die with him, rise with him and enter into eternal life'. This great series of rituals originated in Jerusalem during the third century, when the events leading up to, and including, the suffering, death, resurrection and ascension of Christ were celebrated on their anniversaries and on the very spots where they had originally taken place. All Christian countries soon adopted these solemn rites, adapting them within and without their own churches and cathedrals where, as before, the weekly (Sundays) and later the daily (save Good Friday) masses were the one and only celebration.

The Easter rituals are the external signs of the sacred reality and hold a concept of past, present, and future. Some which still survive commence on Palm Sunday when the community assembles at some distance from the church to await the clergy. All carry palm branches in remembrance of Christ's entry into Jerusalem. The clergy, after blessing the leaves, lead their congregation to the church. Many of these processions in the Middle Ages could be very long, as can be judged by one processional hymn which contained thirty-seven verses to be sung by the clergy, with, after every verse, a chorus to be sung by the common people. (It was composed, in the ninth century, by Bishop Theodulf of Orleans, but only a few verses remain.) The large West door, on this day, is decorated with branches of leaves and flowers, forming a triumphal arch, for all to move under before the celebration of mass within the church.

Maundy Thursday re-enacts the Last Supper—the farewell meal when Christ 'handed' the sacramental rite of his Body and Blood to his disciples, and washed their feet. The mass, including the washing of feet, is celebrated in the evening with all gathered together about one altar. It is the last time the bells of the church will be rung until the end of the Easter Vigil. The altars are stripped of all their furnishings and all the crosses, images and decorations within the church are removed or veiled. Solemn adoration does not continue after midnight.

The sacraments are not celebrated on Good Friday or on the Saturday. The church is empty. On Friday the cross is shown to the people, three times, whilst it is unveiled, and carried in procession to be placed at the entrance to the sanctuary, surrounded by lighted candles. All taking part show their adoration by removing their shoes and walking on their knees to kiss the cross. The cross is then placed on the altar. There are no great processions on this day—there is no consecration, for this day is in memory of a historical event. Communion is distributed—originally only to the people and not the clergy, but from the sixteenth century only to the clergy and *not* the common people. (We read that in the Abbey Church of Durham at the end of the solemn service the cross was carried to a sepulchre, which had been constructed and situated near to the high altar, and placed within it, together with another image of Christ in whose breast had been placed the holy sacrament from the high altar. Two lighted candles were set before the sepulchre to burn until Easter day.)

The church remains empty until Saturday night when begins the festival of fire and light, to end before sunrise on the Sunday morning—the Easter Vigil. All lights in the church are extinguished as a reminder that the Old Law is now at an end. The Church symbolically waits at the Lord's tomb. A large fire (the New Law) is prepared and lit from a flint or rock, away from the church where all the people have gathered awaiting the clergy and the great Paschal Candle. This candle, when unlit, represents the cloud which led the children of Israel by day—the Ancient Law and the Body of Christ—but when lighted it becomes the pillar of fire which was their guide by night, the New Law and the Body of the Risen Christ. This is referred to when the deacon later sings before the lighted candle, with special importance placed upon the likeness of the candle to the body of Christ—the wax was produced by the bee which, like the Virgin, is both chaste and fruitful. The celebrant cuts a cross into the wax and the Greek letters alpha and omega, and lastly the numerals of the current year. He then drives five grains of incense into the candle to give visible expression to the similarity of the wax to the body of Christ to recall the five wounds he suffered and the spices brought by the holy women for his burial. The candle is then lit from the new fire.

The celebrant, the clergy and the congregation now process with the candle to the West door of the church, where the entire assembly light their tapers and candles from the great Paschal Candle before moving into the church to the high altar. All the candles within the church are relit. The celebrant sings the Easter Proclamation ('Exultet') which contains the words 'This is the night where heaven is wedded to earth, and God to man'. Originally the 'Exultet' was improvised by the priest but was later carefully set down. When the 'Gloria' is sung, all the bells are rung in celebration. In joyous procession the congregation, headed by the great candle and those prepared for baptism, move to the baptistry where the font is blessed. The candle is lowered three times into the water symbolizing Christ's baptism, his command 'baptise them in the name of the Father, and of the Son, and of the Holy Spirit', and the mystery of the Holy Spirit entering the water. Baptism follows. The holy water is sprinkled to the four cardinal points, and the week of celebration ends with the mass.

(To end the Durham rituals, two monks took from within the sepulchre an image of Christ with a cross in his hand and the sacrament from the high altar enclosed in crystal within his breast. This was held high for all to see and carried in solemn procession about the entire church. It was then returned to the high altar, there to remain until the day of the Ascension.)

Every moment of the great rituals was really a dramatic presentation with historical meaning. The arrival of the bishop, at the celebration of the mass, symbolised the arrival of Christ. Seven lights carried before him reminded everyone of the seven gifts of the Spirit. In procession, his richly decorated canopy was borne by four representing the Evangelists; two other acolytes 'played the parts' of Moses and Elias. During the first part of the celebration the bishop sat silent, and alone, on his throne recalling by this single dramatic gesture the first years of Christ's life, spent in obscurity and in meditation.

Costume in the Church may have been influenced by Charlemagne, who was crowned by the Pope as Emperor of the Romans in 800 wearing the long Roman tunic, cloak, belt, and richly ornamented sandals. Sandals are seldom richly ornamented today but the basic dress for clergy is otherwise not greatly changed. By the thirteenth century rules governing ecclesiastical vestments were firmly established in opposition to barbaric taste and fashion, including regulations relating to colours and the change of dress during services and feast days. Vestments and ornaments proper to a bishop were and are called 'pontificals' and many of these are again 'representational'. His mitre, with its two points, symbolises knowledge of both the Old and the New Testaments, whilst the two ribbons, falling down the back, state that the interpretation of the scriptures should be by both the letter and the spirit. He wears a ring, usually of pure gold set with a sapphire, on the right hand.

In the early Church, since nothing sacred should be touched by the bare hands, a bishop wore richly decorated and jewelled gloves. His short stockings, of fine material, ended at the knee and were tied with ribbons; his sandals were embroidered and laced. He carried his staff, a crosier or crook often made in gold and elaborately set with precious stones, turning it outwards to denote his authority; when accompanied by an abbot, the abbot covered his staff with a cloth to show that his authority was veiled in the presence of his superior. The pastoral crossed staff of an archbishop was later carried in processions by his chaplain. The throne was also part of the bishop's pontificals.

Any priest vested for mass wears the amice (a hood, now often simply that of his college) with its apparel (embroidery) over the chasuble (a sleeveless robe) decorated with the orphrey (embroidery) over the alb with *its* apparels. The alb is a long tunic, usually of fine white linen, worn by all clergy and also the choristers. The amice was originally a head covering and was thus the first sacred garment to put on; it was worn by all the clergy above the minor orders with an apparel which, when fastened by cords, formed a collar. The chasuble symbolises the charity which is above the precepts of the law, and is in itself the supreme law. Priests higher in rank wore the dalmatic, which had been a fashionable garment worn by upper-class Romans, like the alb but shorter both in its length and sleeves. Still higher in rank, the tunicle is shorter still, and, for symmetry at the altar, worn by both deacon and sub-deacon. During communion, the officiating priest held the maniple, a narrow band of linen first used for wiping the face and hands while serving at the altar, which became a richly decorated piece of embroidery, some three feet in length, carried over the left wrist. The stole (which had been the long robe of Roman matrons), some nine feet in length, was placed over the shoulders of a bishop and hanging loose, but crossed over the chest and tucked under the girdle by lower orders; it is the symbol of the light yoke of the Master and should be cherished and kissed every time the priest puts it on or takes it off. Lastly, everyone had a cope to wear in procession; decorated according to the degree of its wearer, this outer covering with its hood was perhaps the most splendid of all the vestments.

Remembering the profusion of colours in the building itself, and adding the rich colours of the vestments—cathedrals had their own colour symbols and customs, such as blue for Advent, white for Christmas, red for Holy Innocents' Day and Passion Sunday, and, of course, black for funerals—what a sight it must have been for a visitor from the country. Magnificent costume and ornament for magnificent and dramatic celebrations! Medieval man had a strong sense of the magnificence of the world which surrounded him and his faith. He believed in physical and spiritual beauty.

The music, sometimes in the background and sometimes telling part of the service's 'story', became more and more ornamental, too. At solemn service in early Christian history the priests elaborately vocalised and decorated the 'hallelujahs' and 'amens' as show-pieces. Soon these flowery improvisations were given words and by the end of the ninth century they had become long solo songs or short scenes acted out by the choristers or the lower clergy, making clear to the congregation some moment of the drama contained in the service.

The earliest surviving text 'Quem quaeritis' dates from the ninth century. It must have been inserted into Europe's liturgy although the text itself comes from France:

*Angel:*        Whom seek you in the tomb, followers of Christ?

| | |
|---|---|
| *3 Maries:* | Jesus of Nazareth, who was crucified, Oh Dweller in Heaven. |
| *Angel:* | He is not here, He is risen as He foretold; go announce that He is risen from the Sepulchre. |
| *Chorus with Angels:* | Hallelujah! The Lord has risen today, a brave lion. Christ, the Son of God. |
| *Angel:* | Come and see the place where the Lord was laid, Hallelujah! Hallelujah! |
| | Go quickly and tell the disciples that the Lord has risen. Hallelujah! |
| *3 Maries:* | The Lord has hung upon the cross for us, and has risen from the tomb, Hallelujah! |

The earliest extant English text, sung or chanted at the Easter mass, comes from Winchester Cathedral and was prepared by the bishops, abbots and abbesses at the request of King Edgar at a council of Winchester. It is here described by Aethelwold Bishop of Winchester at some time during the middle part of the tenth century. Remember that the entombment of Christ was symbolised by the laying of a cross wrapped in cloth in a special recess in the high altar which was then identified as the Holy Sepulchre:

While the third lesson is being chanted, let four brethren vest themselves. Let one of these vested in an alb enter as though to take part in the service, and let him approach the sepulchre without being observed and let him sit there quietly with a palm in his hand. While the third response is sung, let the remaining three follow, and let them all, vested in copes, bearing in their hands censers and stepping *delicately* as those who seek something, approach the sepulchre. These things are to be done in imitation of the angel sitting in the monument, and the women with spices coming to anoint the body of Jesus. When, therefore, he who sits there beholds the three approach him straying about as if lost and seeking something, let him begin in a dulcet voice of medium pitch to sing 'Whom seek ye in the sepulchre, Oh followers of Christ?' And when he has sung it to the end, let the three reply together 'Jesus of Nazareth who was crucified, Oh celestial One'. Says he 'He is not here, He is risen just as He foretold. Go, announce that He is risen from the dead'. At the word of this bidding let those three turn to the choir and say 'Allelujah! the Lord is risen today. The strong lion, the Christ, the Son of God. Huzza!' This said, let the one still sitting there as if calling them back sing the anthem 'Come and see the place where the Lord was laid. Allelujah! Allelujah!' and saying this let him rise and lift the veil and show them the place bare of the cross, but only the cloths placed there in which the cross was wrapped. And when they have seen this, let them set down their censers which they carried to the sepulchre, and take the cloth and hold it up in the face of the clergy as if to make it known that the Lord has risen and is no longer wrapped therein. Let them then sing the anthem 'The Lord is risen from the Sepulchre, Who for us hung upon the cross', and then lay the cloth upon the altar. When the anthem is done, let the Prior, sharing in their gladness at the triumph of Our King, in that, having conquered death, He rose again, begin the hymn, 'We praise thee, Oh God!' And this begun let *all* the bells chime out together.

Music in the early Church was always a problem to some authoritarian priests who feared that music was too obtrusive and detracted from the spirit of the service. They constantly questioned whether the singers were showing off and if those with fine voices ceased to be interpreters and became performers in their own right. Pope Gregory, who supported a singing school to train boys, had defined plainsong as a guide to the proper use of music (later known as Gregorian chant), but by the tenth century it was no longer 'plain' and by the fourteenth century the plainsong melodies served only as a line on which to hang several pieces of decoration. Plainsong depends entirely on the words of the text.

Very few early folk-songs or words to music, including Church music, have been preserved. Outside church, the pilgrims sang folk hymns to popular tunes (types not unlike the present fashion for 'folky' hymn-singing in schools, accompanied by guitars). Their words were paraphrased directly from the scriptures ('The Word of God') but, with strong influence from the Eastern Church, an increasing number of religious poems were put together and filtered through to the West. Inside church, there was little for the congregation to do. Saint Augustine had said 'Praising without words comes nearer to entertainment than worship' but felt that the feebler members of the congregation would be aroused to some feeling of devotion through singing. For himself he feared that he might be moved more by the beauty of the singers than by their song. But even by the fourteenth century the congregation only joined in a few 'hallelujahs' and chanted the Creed, probably on a single note.

After 1400, music for the mass became a huge structure comparable to the scale of the cathedral in which it was sung. Singing by the choir and soloists occupied every moment, covering the movements of the priest during the service even to the readers of the lessons as they approached to ask for their blessing. Music and song were written to cover the long and great processions on festival days. Words and tunes were changed accordingly to suit certain days of worship in the calendar. Songs to cheer up and give courage to old people or peasants were introduced. The Creed, as the most personal part of the mass, was set to a simple tune so that everyman could sing his own statement of faith.

There were normally five services on weekdays and seven on Sundays. The deacon ('dean') was in charge of all the priests living under the canon (rules) of the cathedral. The cantor (later 'precentor' or first singer) was in charge of musical training. Each dignitary sat immediately behind the choir-screen on opposite sites of the aisle dividing the choir into two antiphonal parts, which bear their original names today: *decani* and *cantoris*. The chancel was for the initiated and their chanting and the nave for the laiety (naïve, or knave?).

Short plays were also written for performance other than for the Easter celebrations. Great crowds assembled on these festival or feast days associating themselves with the clergy and becoming part of the body of Christ. Belief filled the house of worship and in it existed all the arts: architecture; painting and sculpture; the applied arts; music, speech and song; mime and dance.

Man in the Middle Ages lived in a designed universe where all had its appointed place and God's image and mysteries gave order and pattern to everything:

But as it is written, the Eye hath not seen, or ear heard, neither have entered into the heart of man the things which God hath prepared for them that love him. (Corinthians II.9: St Paul's paraphrase of Isaiah LXIV.4.)

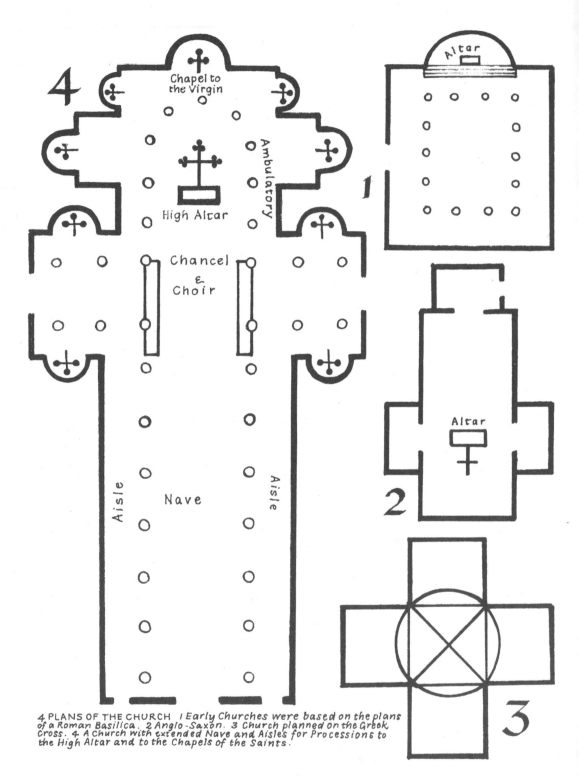

4 PLANS OF THE CHURCH  1 Early Churches were based on the plans of a Roman Basilica. 2 Anglo-Saxon. 3 Church planned on the Greek Cross. 4 A Church with extended Nave and Aisles for Processions to the High Altar and to the Chapels of the Saints.

EAST

north door

principal altar

south door

west door

THE
CHURCH
~ THE
IMAGE
OF CHRIST

Force from above
centering to a
point below

Water

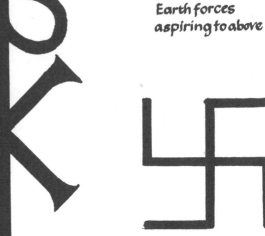

Earth forces
aspiring to above

Rolling Wheel
of the Universe
/positive

THE CRUCIFIXION
or
Symbol of Christ

Rolling Wheel of
the Universe
/negative

A Town defeated

God

Earth

Woman

Man

Greek Cross

6 Pointed Mystic Star
/ solemnity & gladness

The Universe

Clouds

The Earth

EARLY SIGNS & SYMBOLS

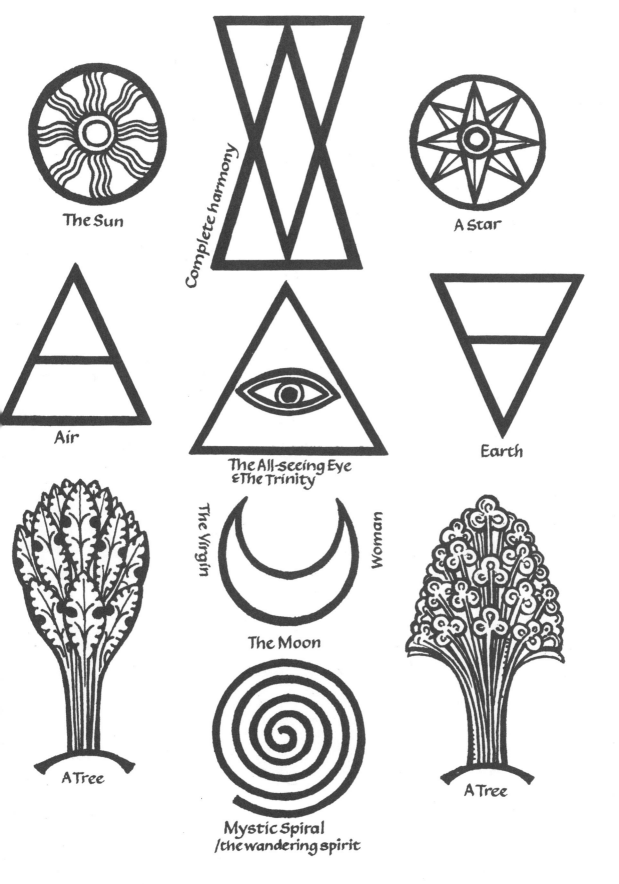

The Sun

Complete harmony

A Star

Air

The All-seeing Eye
& The Trinity

Earth

A Tree

The Virgin

Woman

The Moon

A Tree

Mystic Spiral
/the wandering spirit

EARLY SIGNS & SYMBOLS

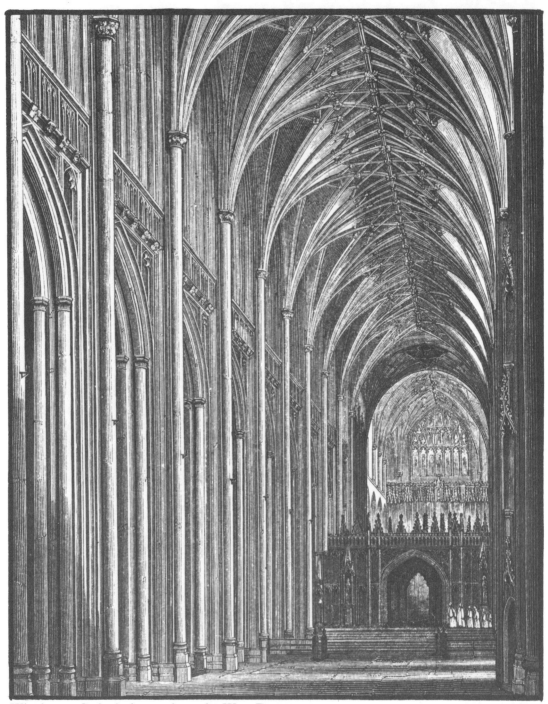

Winchester Cathedral, seen from the West Door

Salisbury Cathedral, seen from the East

47

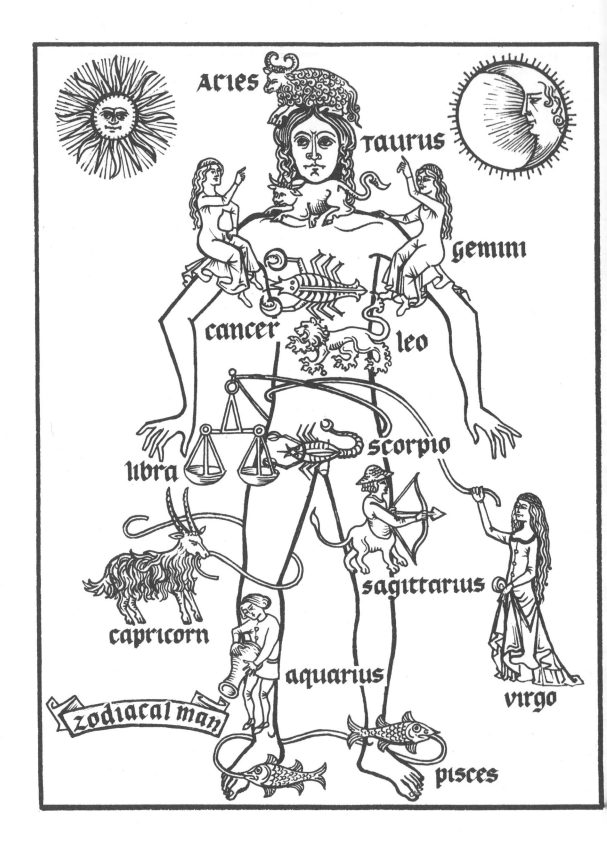

aries

taurus

gemini

cancer

leo

libra

scorpio

sagittarius

capricorn

aquarius

virgo

zodiacal man

pisces

aries

libra

scorpio

sagittarius

taurus

gemini

aquarius

cancer

virgo

pisces

capricorn

signs & symbols of the zodiac

leo

Based on stained glass St Denis

**SYMBOLISM IN THE CHURCH:** Christ crowns the Church and removes the veil that shrouds the Synagogue - the Old & the New. The seven doves represent the seven gifts of the Spirit.

SYMBOLISM IN THE CHURCH: God the Father brings forth his son
from the Ark, in which rests Aaron's rod and the tablets of the law. The
4 symbols of the Evangelists guard, & are the bearers of the Ark.

ADORATION OF
THE VIRGIN

Based on a drawing from the Matthew Paris Chronicles mi3 C3th B.M.

EARLY LITURGICAL DRESS

An Archbishop

An Archbishop

A Priest

A Server

11th

53

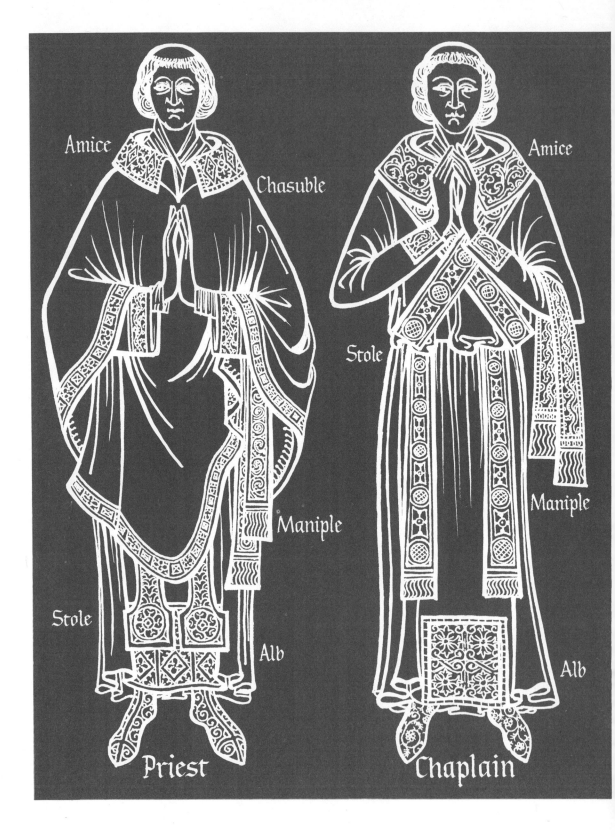

Amice

Chasuble

Maniple

Stole

Alb

Priest

Amice

Stole

Maniple

Alb

Chaplain

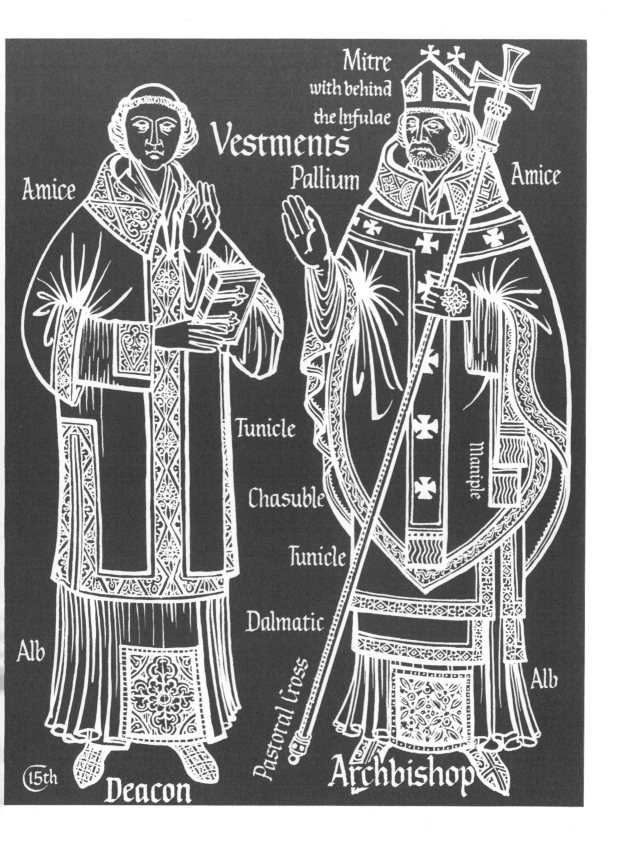

Vestments

Amice

Mitre
with behind
the Infulae

Pallium

Amice

Tunicle

Chasuble

Maniple

Tunicle

Dalmatic

Alb

Alb

Pastoral Cross

15th

Deacon

Archbishop

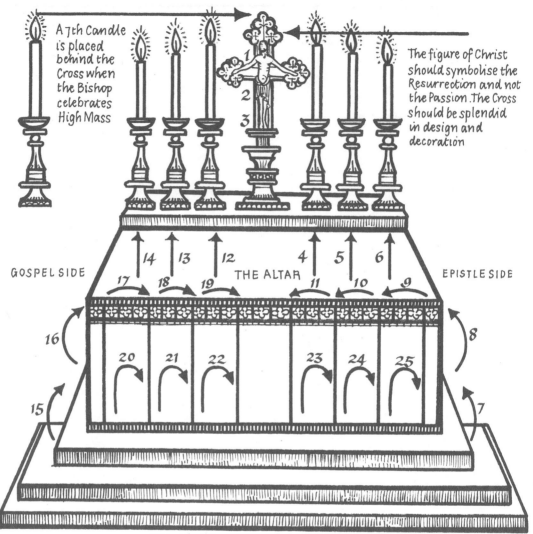

A 7th Candle is placed behind the Cross when the Bishop celebrates High Mass

The figure of Christ should symbolise the Resurrection and not the Passion. The Cross should be splendid in design and decoration

GOSPEL SIDE

THE ALTAR

EPISTLE SIDE

THE ORDER OF INCENSING THE ALTAR

THE TOP OF AN ALTAR (always of stone) SHOWING THE FIVE CROSSES TRACED, BY THE BISHOP WITH HIS THUMB, IN HOLY WATER at the time of consecration

CELEBRATION OF THE MASS c1500

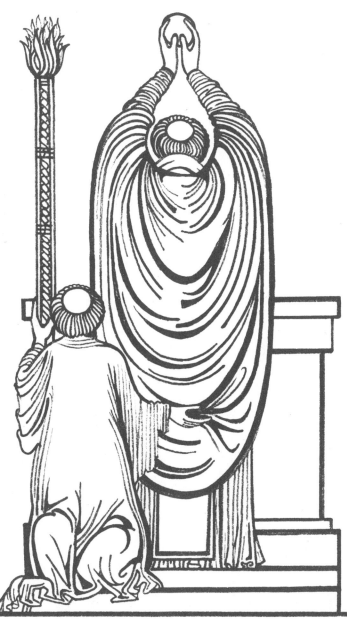

Above: Celebration of the Mass; the elevation of the Host before Communion *after a base relief by Giotto & Pisarro*
Left: Some of the many poses used during the act of communal & private prayer c1200

59

THE MARIES VISITING THE HOLY SEPULCHRE

Based on the Benedictional of St Aethelwold Winchester (10th BM

THE SOLDIERS GUARDING THE HOLY SEPULCHRE

# THE EASTER PLAYS

ST JOHN & ST PETER RUNNING TO THE HOLY SEPULCHRE

# 2

# 𝔍𝔫 𝔱𝔥𝔢 ℭ𝔥𝔲𝔯𝔠𝔥

## *Play-making becomes Ambitious*

Little detailed information is available to determine the style and conventions of presenting medieval religious drama. We have the texts, some
writings, and the fine and applied arts (rarely representing dramatic performances) from which to draw conclusions. However, such information as
there is reveals such a close similarity to the styles employed by classical
Chinese and Japanese theatre that it is worth while examining some of these
Eastern conventions.

The Golden Age of Chinese classical theatre existed some time between
the second half of the fourteenth century and the first half of the seventeenth century. It was an entertainment incorporating as many as forty
short plays, each complete in itself, with a manner of presentation governed
by age-old traditions. Everything was precisely laid down in rule books.
Music, speech, gesture and mime, singing, dancing, acrobatics, costume,
make-up, properties, colours and ornamentation, were all governed by
these books.

Representation and style was symbolic, the story telling direct, simple
and precise. Visually every character was dressed splendidly, were he
peasant or god, and so the understanding of the symbolism required vivid
imagination on the part of the audience. The actors, accompanied by an
orchestra, transported their audience at will (having no scenery in the
accepted sense) through epic countrysides, up hills, across mountains and
down into valleys, crossing lakes and rivers and entering houses—which
are not there! Opening and going through a door is symbolised by simply
opening the hands, from finger-tips touching, to fully outstretched (opening
the door), taking one or two steps and then bringing the finger-tips
together again (walking through the opened door and then closing it). If an
actor continually shrugs his shoulders, he is crying many tears or, should he
hide his face from his audience, he does not exist and is merely the pro-

61

logue. To carry a lighted lantern indicates walking in the dark. A spear thrown by one actor and caught by another tells the audience that the second actor has been killed by the spear. A fan placed beside the face symbolises that the actor is bareheaded and in the sun, whilst a red umbrella, filled with small pieces of white paper and opened up on stage, tells us that the scene is happening in a snow-storm. An actor carrying a whip is riding horseback, and a fly-swat personifies purity (because it recalls the side-to-side movement of censing). Colours of costumes and painted faces carry messages too: white for a wicked man, yellow for marriage; red showing honesty; black, honest but rough; green, evil; and gold is the colour of the heavens and of heavenly beings. So, if two actors meet dressed as warlords—one with a predominantly white make-up and wearing green armour (wickedness and evil) and the other with his face painted in patterns of red (honesty), each having fastened on his back an equal number of flags—the audience has already been informed by costume, make-up, and gesture, that two mighty soldiers meet for a battle, each supported by the same number of men (the flags on their backs represent units of soldiers). Should all these flags be removed from both the warriors, by servants or 'property men', a bloody battle has taken place on stage leaving the two to fight it out alone.

Property men, always dressed in black, and 'non-existent' in the eyes of the audience, rarely leave the stage and continually assist the actor in his stage tasks, helping to remove parts of the splendid costume or spreading cushions on the carpet covering the acting area (the last to set a death scene or a moment when a character wants to go to sleep). They also make tea to give to the actors when they have completed their work and are sitting quietly ready for their next entrance. These stage servants are also present to indicate a change of place. Flags or strips of painted silk, held up and carrying decorative emblems, immediately represent seas, the sky, forests, and countryside. Two property men, walking on either side of an actor, each holding a small white flag decorated with a simple wheel describe, with the utmost simplicity, the fact that the actor is travelling in his coach or chariot. When they leave the actor, and return to their places at the sides of the stage, we know that the stage character has got out of his chariot and is now walking. If he changes his rhythm of walk to high stepping, he is going upstairs; if he walks round and round in decreasing circles, he is climbing a hill. Chinese theatre is childlike in its simple beauty of imaginative story-telling.

Similar skills and conventions can also be found in the Japanese popular theatre *(Kabuki)* and in the *Noh* drama with its even stricter formality and rule-books. The secrets of Noh playing were guarded until the beginning of this century. Every moment and method of expression from preparation to completion of a performance has its order and ritual. A pebble path running parallel to the front of the elevated stage must be laid out before each performance; like the flight of steps which lead from it to the stage floor, this is never used but is a reminder that the plays were originally given under the roof of a shrine or temple. The costumes are unpicked and taken to pieces after being used, carefully folded, and put into fine lacquered boxes. 'We begin with nothing and end with nothing.'

Preparing and dressing the actors is a long and formal procedure, for each actor has a clearly defined number of assistants or dressers according to his place in the company. On stage too, the sections of the play are rigidly designed with specific placings for each actor: when the *shi-te* enters through a curtained door, all the other actors must retreat from those areas which are reserved for him alone. The curtain is then held up by two poles to form a canopy down a 'bridge' *(hashigakari)* to the stage. Three fronds of pine (important markers) are set at intervals along the hashigakari and a scenic pine tree decorates the back of the stage (indicating superior spiritual qualities). Everything on stage has its meaning as the shi-te's performance develops into speech, song, mime, gesture and dance.

The play is accompanied by a chorus sitting stage left and a group of musicians who sit stage right. At the back of the stage, remaining silent throughout, sits an old man: once one of the company's leading actors, he is there to see that all is kept in proper order. Noh served the 'proper orders' only—the nobility and *samurai*—and was understood only by members of that order.

'Forget the theatre and look at the Noh.
Forget the Noh and look at the actor.
Forget the actor and look at the idea.
Forget the idea and you understand Noh.'

Early Christian drama must have required similar training of the voice and a strong technique in mime and gesture from its actors. One Latin play mentioned by Karl Mantzius, *Planctus Marias et Aliorum*, includes clear instructions for the actors to adopt.

*Magdalena :*    Oh, brothers,
    (Magdalena shall turn towards the men with out-
    stretched arms)
    Oh, sisters,
    (She turns to the women)
    Where is my hope?
    (She beats her breast)
    Where is my consolation?
    (She lifts her hands)
    Where is all my salvation, Oh, my Master?
    (She bends her head and throws herself at the
    feet of Christ)

*The Virgin Mary :*    Oh, pain!
    (Mary wrings her hands)
    Oh, pain! Why,
    Oh, beloved Son,
    (Opens her hands and points towards Christ)
    Dost thou hang thus,
    Thou, who art life,
    And has been from the beginning.
    (Beats her breast)

We learn that 'Adam should be trained to speak and gesture at the right moment and not to be late or too soon. All should be practised in speaking calmly and making appropriate movements to fit with the words.' These early plays are full of simple yet evocative stage directions, like 'Abel shall have a saucepan beneath his garment against which Cain shall knock when he pretends to kill Abel who shall then lie full out as if he were dead', or 'a chair representing Jerusalem shall be placed on a suitable spot and on this chair the high priest shall stand, whilst on another chair shall stand Saint Paul. On either side, and at a distance, two chairs are to represent Damascus, and Judas shall be seated on one of them and the other shall be occupied by the senior member of the synagogue.'

Costumes and properties are equally carefully recorded. *Peregrimi*, performed on the Monday of Passion Week and played in England (though the existing text, like so many others, comes from Northern France), requires the minor clergy to be dressed in tunics and copes and to carry staffs and purses as travellers, with caps on their heads and bearded. A priest barefooted, and clothed in alb and amice, and bearing a cross upon his right shoulder, and with a down-cast countenance, should move up to them down the right aisle of the church. A 'mansion' or stage prepared in the likeness of the village of Emmaus, is to be set in the middle of the nave, with a table placed there for the Lord and his disciples. Elsewhere, it is recorded that 'watchers', dressed as soldiers, kept vigil all night on the steps leading up to the Easter Sepulchre singing psalms. The steps were covered with black cloth and on each step were placed fine silver candlesticks holding lighted waxen candles. We read of a 'manger to be placed at the back of the altar' or of 'many boys dressed as angels sitting high in the roof of the church', and of 'two clerics dressed in dalmatics to represent midwives who draw aside a curtain to reveal the infant Christ'. This was the highly symbolic Christian equivalent of the Chinese and Noh plays, enacted in early Norman cathedrals.

Japanese Kabuki, on the other hand, is a mixture of many styles reminiscent of late medieval and Elizabethan playing, at one moment formal and highly stylised and the next moment very realistic. Kabuki is full of magical enchantment, with elaborate use of stage scenery and mechanical devices. Actors, fantastically dressed and made up, dancers, musicians, chorus and property men are often all on stage at the same time.

One remarkable moment of Kabuki magic is performed by the *onnagata* or player of female roles (all parts are played by men), in no way resembling 'drag' technique but creating with the utmost delicacy the essence of maidenhood. The actor glides on stage with tiny steps, looking like a fragile piece of porcelain, knees brushing together, and with the eyes cast modestly downwards to the ground, the long 'weeping' sleeves covering her hands, the face ivory white. The story requires that 'she' be transformed into a spider. 'She' turns her back to the audience, the property men move forward, ribbons are undone. The costume changes shape and colour from a soft, sinuous ripple of whites and pearly tones into a massive bulk of reds, purples and gold (springs have been concealed in the original garments to be released by her attendants). The young girl's wig, too, has its springs and coils, and on the release of more silk ties it leaps out into a great mane of black hair. At the same time another property man has been repainting her face from a small palette of colours and brush. In less than a minute the transformation is complete. 'She' turns with violent and stamping steps, and with grunting and low bellowing sounds reveals a hideous and violent mask of spirals and swirls painted in black, red and white. Spreading her arms wide, 'she' releases from between each finger red streamers, flinging them high into the air. For some few seconds we see a great royal spider centred in its own web. How near did the boys playing female parts in medieval mysteries come to these techniques?

A mixture of realism and cunning naturalism in one Kabuki play, using skilful tricks, shows a complete Caesarian operation, performed in full view of the audience and terminating with the birth of the child: how many nativity plays may have used similar tricks? Another piece of imaginative realism is well illustrated, in a sequence from a very long play, when a faithful samurai has to leave his palace. The stage is bare of representational scenery, other than a large formal painting some twenty-five or more feet across, at the back of the stage, depicting a palace. The actor indicates to his audience that he is weeping and starts to leave the stage by means of the *hanamichi*, which, unlike the hashikagari of Noh, is a long bridge or walk from the back of the audience to the stage. He proceeds some twelve feet or so but has suggested by his rhythm of walk a distance of perhaps half a mile. At this moment the back wall, with its representation of the palace, falls forward on to the stage revealing an identical picture behind it but with the representation now only half its original size. The samurai executes another dozen or so paces and yet again the back wall drops forward, this time showing the palace occupying only a very small central area of the final cloth. The actor, who is now almost at the back of the theatre, makes his exit, never to return. Symbolism and scene-painter have combined with the actor's skill to transport the audience's imagination miles in time and distance in the matter of minutes. How many 'prodigal sons' or banished kinsmen in English plays may have left by similar means?

The Kabuki actor is attended, just like the Noh player, the performer in the Chinese classical theatre, and the Christian priest during solemn service, by his assistants or helpers. In Japanese theatre they were probably originally the manipulators of the old puppet plays, dressed in their black uniforms and hooded, to all intent and purpose non-existent, not unlike the Black Theatre of Prague today. The puppet, skilfully worked by three or more 'shadows' or servants servile to the life of their doll, appears more real than real, controlling the manipulators, sometimes even showing impatience that they should all apply themselves harder to their work! The 'shadows' wander in and out of Kabuki playing (after all, they are not really there), perhaps to repair a piece of shaky scenery, arriving complete with step-ladder, nails and hammer. They change the setting, prompt, and even cover for an actor who has lost his lines. Convention allows for the mystical word 'imagination', for 'we are all but shadows' and can share a world where reason does not interfere with magic.

This 'popular' Japanese theatre, with its mechanical tricks and contrived realism, may have supported the later Elizabethan theatre but it may well also—however remotely—show us how some early church performances drew their public. An Easter play, the text originally coming from Orleans but without doubt performed in England, includes in the action the visit of the three women to the tomb, and the race of Saint Peter and Saint John to the Holy Sepulchre, running down the whole length of the nave on hearing the good news of Christ's Resurrection. John was clothed in a white tunic and carried a palm frond in his hand whilst Peter brought the keys and was dressed in red. (A race of this kind was later heavily criticised by a sixteenth century English gentleman as unseemly, showing that drama within the church was still being performed during the reign of Elizabeth I.) An angel clothed in a golden alb and wearing a coif spoke in 'a modulated and grave voice', holding in his left hand a palm frond and in his right a candelabrum full of lighted candles. Two angels were discovered inside the sepulchre (here a curtain may have been pulled aside or there may have been doors), and on the arrival of one dressed in the likeness of a gardener the angels left the sepulchre to be seen by all. They were instructed to unfold a muslin cloth: 'These are the clothes of the blessed body, which lay abandoned in the empty tomb'. Then they placed the clothes upon the altar: 'God of Gods has risen today'. The priest who appeared as the gardener returned in the likeness of the Lord dressed in a dazzling white robe with a precious phylacterium (mitre) and white infulae upon his head. He carried in his left hand a pall, to be woven of gold, which was used to cover the sacramental chalice before and after the mass, and in his right hand he held a cross bearing on it ⚶—his mystic symbol.

Mechanical scene devices were frequently used. One text demands an overhead cable from which, hanging from a cord, a star is suspended, capable of moving backwards and forwards. It also asks for a manger and for the appearance of angels from 'aloft'. Lines invite the standing congregation to worship the infant Christ. The Magi enter, each from a different part of the church ('as if from their own lands') and meet before the altar. The star moves forward ('let them follow coming to the entrance of the choir') and they depart ('let the star go before them which has not yet appeared in the sight of Herod'). The Kabuki 'exit' routine would have been valuable here.

A similar overhead device is still to be seen today during Easter celebrations in Florence. The ceremony is called *Scoppio del Carro*. A dove on a wire, stretching from the high altar of the cathedral, through the cathedral, and outside to a float filled with fireworks in the square below, is set off on its journey by a firework fixed to its body and on its arrival it sparks off the fireworks and blows up the float. (In Old Saint Paul's, London, on Whit Monday, a dove was let down through a hole in the roof, with burning tow, to represent the tongues of fire alighting on the apostles.) In Italy from the fourteenth century onwards many elaborate scenic effects for church plays and celebrations were both splendid and spectacular. In one such effect twenty-one boys, dressed as angels, descended in a machine from the roof of the church, a 'sky above a great stage, in which wheels, constructed as if in the air, move from the centre to the edges in most beautiful order, ten orbits for the ten heavens all full of little lamps representing stars'. Clouds descended full of fire, and thunderbolts came from on high. These must have been 'represented' as were the wheels of the Chinese chariot (see page 62).

Soon after the introduction of dramatic scenes within the church service, these short playlets were removed from the service proper to be performed independently (in detached scenes—one represented a symbolic re-enactment of the Massacre of the Innocents) or in groups at matins, vespers, or on special feast days. From the twelfth century, groups of these plays (linked together to form a common theme) were acted by younger members of the clergy—particularly on the sixth of December, the eve or day of Saint Nicholas, the patron saint of scholars. All dramatic representation was directly based on the Bible, or, at a slightly later date, on stories of the lives of saints and martyrs. The productions were developed more in Europe than in England, though there was one Geoffrey, from the University of Paris, arriving at Saint Albans as a candidate for master of the abbey school, who, having failed to obtain his post, went to Dunstable and attempted to present a miracle play called *Santa Katarina*. (In 1119 he was elected abbot!)

The language of the plays moved gradually from Latin to the vernacular and was either chanted or sung, or both, sometimes accompanied with music—sometimes without. The performers were not professional actors but devout priests, and sometimes nuns, who had to develop a simple and direct skill in gesture and speech to communicate their stories from the Old and the New Testaments to their congregations. The professional actors of the late Middle Ages must have been influenced by some of these techniques.

The original focal point for presentation was the high altar or a specially built 'sepulchre' for the Easter plays. But with plays linked together and requiring different places of action to tell the story more fully, the whole of the church was slowly brought into use. Stages (stages of development of the story and the changing locale, usually referred to as 'houses' or 'mansions') were placed around the perimeter of the church and in its midst, allowing for continuous performance from one stage to the next. The player-clergy moved through the standing congregation from one defined place of action (as with Noh plays) to another. The mansions were simple structures, symbolising such places as Heaven, the house of the Maries or the disciples, Emmaus, Galilee, Hell or a jail, and so forth. They were most probably set upon little platforms, with a short flight of steps leading up from the floor of the church (as with the Kabuki *hanamichi*, see page 66) to elevate the actor from his audience.

Seating for an audience/congregation is a relatively new luxury and comfort. People stood and enjoyed or endured long services and sermons. They would shift and adapt their position around and about the church, according to the stage or stages occupied by the actors, as a crowd moves around listening to the various orators at Speakers' Corner in Hyde Park today. The central area of the nave, where the people stood, could also have been used as an unlocalised area of action or 'no-man's-land', entered or crossed by an actor to symbolise a long journey, a street, or a desert.

Before long, elements of comedy or 'funny business' found their way into the plays. The merchant who sold ointment to the Maries reflects the character of the typical shopkeeper who was to be seen in his shop in the street outside the church, and there is a play in which Herod interrupts the service by throwing a spear at the choir whilst his attendants attack the bishop, canons, and choristers with inflated bladders. Laughter and lusty behaviour was good therapy for these devout Christians whose lives were often precarious for fear of famine, sickness, plague and war.

The Church introduced special festivals and entertainments given over to burlesque, satire and broad comedy within its walls—should not God's house contain everything? The ornament certainly did so: in Wells Cathedral there is a stone carving of a man in great pain with the toothache in the south transept, and a woman with the same malady is represented in the north. A capital to a column in the cathedral of Strasbourg shows, in a burlesque representation, the funeral of a hedgehog borne to the grave by other animals whilst a stag says mass and an ass chants from a reading desk. 'The Feast of the Boy Bishop', 'The Feast of Fools' and 'The Feast of Asses' were regular, though suspect, festivals held both in England and France. They were no doubt based on the old Roman Saturnalia when the masters and their servants changed roles.

'The Feast of the Boy Bishop' disappeared in England during the Reformation. In 1541 a proclamation forbade gatherings by children 'decked and apparelled to counterfeit priests, bishops and women' on 'Saint Nicholas, Saint Catherine, Saint Clement, the Holy Innocents, and such like' and also singing masses and preaching by boys on those days. It is easy to see why the festival began at regular service with 'He hath put down the mighty from their seat and hath exalted the humble and the meek'. The lower clergy and the young choristers at this moment took over from their superiors, and revelry began. At Salisbury there were elaborate regulations. 'The Bishop' might perform the office, but could not hold a banquet or entertain a visitor within or without the cathedral. He could be invited to the table of a canon but he had to return to his duties in church and school immediately after the feast of the Innocents.

The first day of January, the Feast of the Circumcision, was the day for 'The Feast of Fools and Asses'. An ass was an essential feature of the festival as a parody based on the Lord's triumphant entry into Jerusalem. We know that it was performed at Lincoln, Beverley, and at Old Saint Paul's, disappearing in the fourteenth century to be replaced by the 'King or Lord of Misrule' who was appointed to oversee Christmas celebrations at court, colleges, and at universities. But the 'Ass' festival continued well into the seventeenth century.

In the more amusing accounts from France (though there is no reason to suppose England was any different) the 'King' or 'Boy Bishop' arrived on a donkey and clerics were baptised with buckets of water. At Beauvais, there were drinking bouts in the porch of the cathedral and censing with pudding and sausage. In 1264 we read of the 'Bishop' and the 'Dean of Fools' taking part in the services, censing in comic fashion, braying and howling the entire office. Jean Charlier de Gerson (1400), Rector of Paris University, denounced 'the indecencies of the feast that would put to shame a kitchen or a tavern. The Chapters will do nothing to stop them and if the bishops protest they are insulted and taken no notice of. Interposition of Royal authority is needed.' In 1445 the dean of the faculty of theology writes frantically to the bishops and chapters of France concerning the behaviour of 'Priests and clerks who may be seen wearing masks and gross visages during the hours of office. They dance in the choir . . . While the celebrant is singing mass they sing wanton songs and eat black pudding at the corner of the altar. They play dice there. They cense with the stinking smoke from shoes. They leap and run through the church with no sense of their own shame. They drive about the town and its theatres in old carts and wagons and cause laughter from their fellows and onlookers with their infamous performances of obscenely abusive verses, accompanied with indecent gesturings.' In reality it was probably no more than a 'rag' week, as is still known in some university towns.

The licensed fool who took part in many of these ceremonies must not be confused with the town or village fool—a member of the community who, it was believed, was endowed with purity and insight. The licensed or the professional fool wore parti-coloured clothes and a cap with horns or asses' ears upon his head. Bells decorated his garments and he carried, as his weapon, a baton topped with a 'Mr Punch' head, or an inflated bladder full of dried beans or peas, or a wooden sword. A tumbler and acrobat, his costume, bawdy humour, and the animal symbols all suggest that he was originally part of an early pagan folk festival. Making somewhat less awesome a sudden encounter with the 'Devil' or 'Death' in the street plays soon to follow, in these early festivals he often accompanied the Devil as his comic servant or 'Vice'.

'The Dance of Death' was very popular. It was a kind of pantomime composed of music, dance and singing, and is recorded as having been performed in Paris, by order of the English who were then masters there, in 1424. Possibly originating from the Low Countries, it was an allegorical representation of Death leading a cross-section of humanity in a dance to the grave and a constant reminder also of the terrible mortality rate of the dreaded plague attacking all, no matter be they rich or poor, with no pardon. Clerics, knights, popes, ladies, whores, scholars, judges, peasants, beggars, children, kings and emperors, nuns, merchants, and many more were represented. A contemporary wall painting in the cloisters of Old Saint Paul's Cathedral (paid for by John Carpenter, then town clerk of London) illustrated the dance, with written statements and answers coming from the mouths of the dancers and the mouth of Death.

The dance was performed in the streets or in the town square in front of the cathedral and it is unlikely that it was ever performed by members of the clergy. It was surely part of a professional company's repertoire.

The elders of the Church were showing concern, morally and ethically, about the growth and popularity of dramatic and satiric representations of the scriptures within its sacred buildings. Priests were occupying themselves in play-making, when perhaps their time should have been spent on less questionable pursuits. Who knows? Anyhow, the authorities now decided to disassociate themselves from performances of plays within their walls and orders were passed to prohibit drama and entertainment in the church itself, and to make their organisation and presentation the responsibility of the townspeople, and in particular, the guilds. Many of the clergy, however, still found time or excuses to pursue their histrionic talents and, from evidence, we still hear of them performing in the street presentations now to follow.

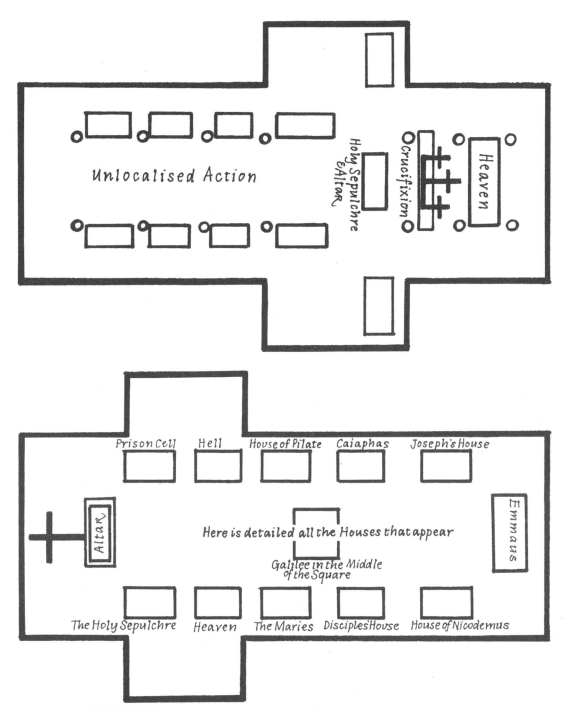

Unlocalised Action

Holy Sepulchre Altar

Crucifixion

Heaven

Prison Cell    Hell    House of Pilate    Caiaphas    Joseph's House

Altar

Here is detailed all the Houses that appear

Galilee in the Middle of the Square

Emmaus

The Holy Sepulchre    Heaven    The Maries    Disciples' House    House of Nicodemus

2 VARIATIONS FOR THE SETTING OF MANSIONS WITHIN THE CHURCH IN READINESS FOR PERFORMANCE OF THE EASTER PLAYS

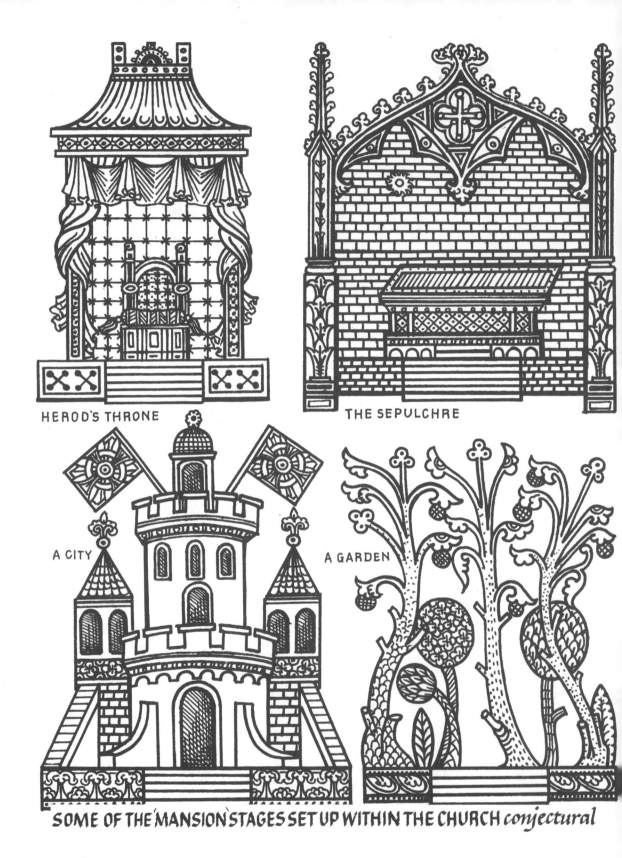

HEROD'S THRONE

THE SEPULCHRE

A CITY

A GARDEN

SOME OF THE 'MANSION' STAGES SET UP WITHIN THE CHURCH *conjectural*

THE CHRISTMAS PLAYS · The Birth of Jesus: The Angel appearing before the Shepherds; & the Magi, guided by the star, bringing their gifts to the Child. 12th

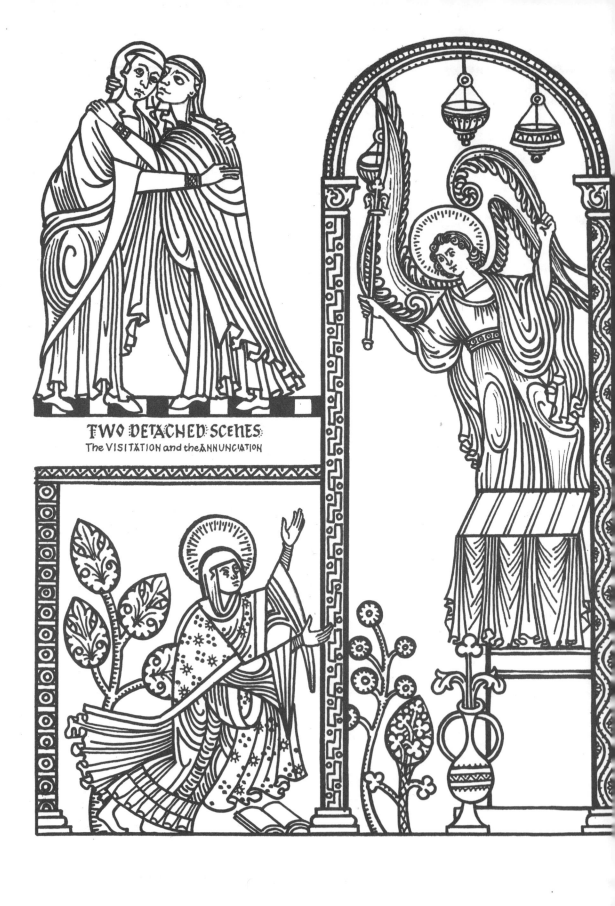

TWO DETACHED SCENES
The VISITATION and the ANNUNCIATION

DETACHED SCENES
St JOHN'S VISION & HIS DEATH

Based on Stained Glass from LYON S

A DETACHED SCENE - THE BAPTISM OF CHRIST

A DETACHED SCENE - THE ASCENSION OF CHRIST

THE FOOL IN THE STREETS

AS THE SERVANT OF THE DEVIL

THE FOOL—IN EOUT OF THE CHURCH Based on 15th & 16th woodcuts

Priests consorting with travelling players ﹙15th

Part of a Dance of Death

An Abbess, Jester, Courtesan
& Knight being led to their deaths c1530

# 3

# In the Streets and the Town Square

## *Commercial Theatre*

Some time between 1200 and 1300 the plays left the church to be performed in the town square. The reason for this development can be related to two facts. The first was the ecclesiastical doubt as to the correctness of clergy dressing up and appearing in plays; and the second was that the increasing population of the townsfolk made it impossible to get them into the church all at the same time to witness the religious plays, which were getting more and more ambitious both in their staging and in the number of scenes which were required to be represented.

From Rome in 1210, Pope Innocent III ordered that the plays should be presented outside the church. Pope Urban, in the year 1264, determined the day of their performance—they were to be held on the Thursday after Trinity Sunday (Corpus Christi). The higher clergy gave constant warnings to priests that they should not take part in the staging of sacred subjects outside the church, and by doing so encouraged the local people to take over the organisation of dramatic festivals.

Mystery plays were concerned with biblical themes, especially the events connected with the birth, life, death and resurrection of Christ. Miracle plays portrayed the lives of the saints and the martyrs, biblical and post-biblical. 'Mystery' as a term serves for both types of plays in England. When banished from the church, the mystery plays moved first to the churchyard, where fairs and markets were originally held, then on to the town square, and sometimes even to the tavern yard. They developed into the great 'Cycle' which tells the story from the Creation to the Day of Judgement, right through from the Old Testament to the Resurrection of Christ, sometimes lasting for as long as seven days in performance. The earliest cycles date from around the beginning of the reign of Edward III in the fourteenth century and are last heard of at the time of James I, the early seventeenth century. At first they were played by priests, boys, and occasionally nuns, but were soon given over to the townspeople and the guilds.

The West porch of a church offered a fine formal background with its carvings of the evangelists, the saints, kings and martyrs, Christ in Majesty and the Last Judgement. The linked scenes now spread out into a straight line, each 'mansion' or station a little distant from the next, and began to be set in their correct order on a long platform stage running the full width of the square. This stationary presentation was very popular in France, especially in Valenciennes where the long stage accommodated eight mansions or settings: Hell's Mouth with a torture chamber, a lake with a boat, the Gates of Paradise, a bishop's house, a castle, Jerusalem, a temple, and Nazareth. The front part of the stage, nearest to the audience, was used for action not requiring any specific locale. Although popular in Europe we find little record of this method of platform staging being employed in England, though it may have been used at Coventry from time to time. A passion play presented once in every ten years at Oberammergau, a village in Bavaria, uses this static form of playing. It has now become highly commercial in its vast undertaking, drawing tourists from all over the world, perhaps not entirely dissimilar in its objectives to the city guilds which organised the cycle plays in the High Middle Ages.

It is possible, then, to assume that in England when the plays left the church the positioning of the mansions was very similar to their placings in the church, either forming a semicircle, or three sides of a square, or even a circle *or* square with some mansions in the centre. The audience would have occupied the inner area and the performers moved through them from one stage to the next.

A vigorous relationship grew up between actor and audience containing, no doubt, much improvised action and dialogue when the performers were confronted by noisy and cheeky spectators, some home from war, and including apprentices, workers, beggars, cutpurses and the professional ladies. Once the drama left the church, the characters and the content of the plays became less formal. Local customs, words, humour, accents, and impersonations of the local dignitaries were slowly woven into the fabric of the performances. Strange 'Eastern' characters mingled with the English craftsmen who acted in them and for whose edification they were written. A strong mixture of formal and symbolic representation contrasted with native boisterousness, good humour, local songs, dances, and naturalness. Styles changed constantly in acting, speech, movement and in the use of scenery and elaborate costumes. Each scene, each character (independent of the whole) combined to tell the story as simply and as directly as possible.

The market square was the town centre. Here stood the great mother church and the town hall, the clock, the gallows, stocks and the whipping post. Public punishment was another form of popular entertainment. Men were accustomed to seeing traitors hanged, drawn and quartered, heretics burnt at the stake alive, and the cutting off of ears, feet or hands. Sheep-stealers had their hands cut off. For speaking evil the tongue was cut out. 'Let the punishment fit the crime!' Burglars were buried alive and if a woman poisoned her husband she was burned alive. 'The greatest and most grievous punishment used in England for those who offend against the state is the drawing from the prison to the place of execution upon an hurdle or sled, where they are hanged till they be half dead and then taken down and quartered alive . . . their members and bowels are cut from their bodies and thrown into a fire provided near at hand and within their own sight, even for the same purpose.' Music often accompanied such an execution.

In the square traders set up their open stalls, buying and selling on market days. Here were held the fairs on feast days. Here the soldiers were trained . . . and here also performed the strolling players, the entertainers and the vagabonds.

The individual plays, from the traditional periods of Christmas and Easter and from other days in the Church's calendar (as many as fifty), arranged and played one after the other in chronological sequence of events, became the occasion for a great holiday and civic pride in many English towns. Once the scheme and organisation had been established, the new sequences of presentation (peculiar to England) became known as 'cycle plays'. Amongst those few surviving are the cycles of York (54 plays), Coventry (43), Chester (25) and Wakefield (32). The full list will never be known: Beverley had a cycle of 36, Newcastle-upon-Tyne and Norwich 12 each, but hundreds of other villages and towns combined to create their own cycles of plays. There was hardly a town in the British Isles which did not have at least one play of its own to be performed in the square, church-yard or streets.

In 1411 the City of London cycle 'From the beginning of the World' was played continually for seven days. No copy of these plays remains, but we know that the performances began at sunrise and lasted until torch-bearers were called out at dusk to stand at the foot of the wagons which served as stages. Each play was taken around the town to be presented at various places where people could gather during the course of the day. This method of presentation probably started in imitation of the Corpus Christi procession, when a large body of ecclesiastics, worshippers, and religious organisations followed the Host around from one church to the next. By now the number of plays had also outgrown the confines of the town square, and sister churches in other parts of the town provided other locations. At the conclusion of the performance, the mother church presented a small Annunciation play, performed by two choristers *inside* the mother church—in the case of London, St Paul's—in front of the high altar.

The guilds were the only organised body within the city, other than the Church. They were very powerful, sometimes tyrannical, and all trades, merchants, skilled workers, and apprentices, were controlled by them. They covered almost every trade and profession, among them carpenters, pouch-makers, cappers and hatters, dyers, silversmiths and goldsmiths, wire-setters, glovers, tailors, and weavers. So no cycle of plays could be put together without their crafts and skills, and in the control the Church had to give them for the organisation and staging of all religious drama, they no doubt saw splendid advertising and commercial possibilities! The guilds gave importance and fame to their towns through vigorous trading and pride in the quality of craftsmanship, skills and produce. Each trade had its own street—Shoe Lane, Mincing Lane, Leather Lane, Pudding Lane, Thread-needle Street, Butter Walk, Broad Street (where sheep and cows were sold), Slaughter Lane, etc. Shops were identified by the hanging sign outside their place of business.

The guilds owned considerable property, they cared for their members, their widows and children and orphans, and many set up schools. Originally they were religious and charitable organisations gathering about them men of similar interests, thoughts and craft. By the fifteenth century in London, they had their own halls and their own churches or chapels, contributing handsomely to their upkeep and commissioning stained glass windows, vestments, church furniture, altar cloths and hangings. They encouraged finery and display and vied with each other in putting on the best show. Their big chance of the year came on the days when the great Cycle was performed and they presented their 'pageants'. Each play had its own horse-drawn 'pageant wagon'—usually a four- or six-wheeler—to move the play on to the next stopping-place within the town. These wagons were two-storied. The lower storey was curtained off and used as a retiring and changing place for the actor, and the upper storey, reached by a ladder or through a trap-door, was set with its own particular mansion or scenery. Most of the action took place on the higher level. The leading actors on leaving the 'tiring house' often mingled with their audience before ascending the ladder to make a formal entrance. Other actors probably remained on the stage, forming a tableau, whilst they were carted on to their next station, like the floats in the Lord Mayor's Show which the City of London still stages once a year.

The banner of the guild was carried in front of its own wagon for the purpose of identification and was no doubt useful too as a means of good publicity. Each guild tried to choose a play associated with its craft or business. Here are some obvious examples:

Bakers: *The Last Supper*
Fishmongers: *The Feeding of the Five Thousand*
Winemakers: *The Wedding at Cana*
(All these three plays allowed the guild to give away samples to the audience.)
Armourers: *Adam and Eve driven from Eden by a Sword*
The Tile Thatchers of York: *The Birth of Jesus*
(Their craft was shown in the construction of the barn roof where Jesus was born.)

Two other guild's choices give us interesting glimpses of their staging:

### Dyers: *Pharaoh*

From a Guild account we read, 'Item: paid for halfe a yard of Red Sea'. This charming yet very important piece of information gives us clues as to the style and manner of performance. The half-yard of red cloth representing the Red Sea would be held up by two servants, to be parted by the actor playing Moses, who would then pass on his way between the two, symbolising that the Red Sea had been safely crossed. Note how clearly this recalls the Chinese classical theatre.

### The Water-leaders and Drawers in Dye: *The Deluge*

The beasts and fowls may have been painted on and around the Ark, but it is pleasanter to think in terms of a scroll, with all the creatures painted on it in correct order, being unwound by the actors as they each say their few lines:

| | |
|---|---|
| *Shem :* | Sir, here are lions, leopards in, |
| | Horses, mares, oxen and swine, |
| | Goats, calves, sheep and kine, |
| | Here sitten may you see. |
| *Ham :* | Camels, asses, men may find; |
| | Buck, doe, hart and hind, |
| | And beasts of all manner kind. |
| | Here be, as thinks me. |
| *Japhet :* | Take here cats and dogs too, |
| | Otter, fox, fulmart also; |
| | Hares, hopping gaily, can ye |
| | Have kail here to eat. |
| *Noah's wife :* | And here are bears, wolves set, |
| | Apes, owls, marmoset; |
| | Weasels, squirrels, and ferret |
| | Here they eat meat. |
| *Shem's wife :* | Yet mote beasts are in this house! |
| | Here cats come in full crowse, |
| | Here a rat and here a mouse; |
| | They stand nigh together. |
| *Ham's wife :* | And here are fowls less and more, |
| | Herons, crane and bittern; |
| | Swans, peacocks, have them before! |
| | Meat for this weather. |
| *Japhet's wife :* | Here are cocks, kites, crows, |
| | Rooks, ravens, many rows; |
| | Cuckoos, curlews, who so knows, |
| | Each one in his kind. |
| | And here are doves, ducks, drakes, |
| | Redshanks, running through the lakes, |
| | And each fowl that language makes |
| | In this ship men may find. |

Over fifty creatures are mentioned by name in this Chester text, which also has the delightful stage direction that Noah is to let down a dove with an olive branch in its mouth 'on a string'.

The texts of some of these plays suggest that four different acting areas could be used to give logic to the story: if God was required to be seen sitting in his Majesty, a little tower was added, raising him some four or five feet above the normal acting level of the upper storey; the lower storey, generally curtained off, could then represent Hell, a dungeon or the interior of the ark etc; and the actors also used the area surrounding the wagon to mingle with their audience and move towards the stage as if coming from far distant lands.

Stage settings were at times very elaborate. At Coventry, for example, they had a 'Hell-Mouth' which had a windlass and a means of showing fire belching out of the mouth, a barrel to simulate the booming sound of an earthquake, and an apparatus 'for setting three worlds afire'. Many stage effects aimed for realism as well as symbolic representation, such as the severed head of Saint Peter which jumped three times on the stage and 'at each jump there flowed a fountain'; the Holy Ghost which descended in fire (possibly with the help of ignited alcohol), and an unfortunate saint whose breasts (made of papier mâché?) were cut off. In one play where a group of monks were to be martyred, a baker put some dough into the baking chamber and to prove that the oven was really hot, reopened the door and brought out a new loaf. Some stage-hand inside the oven obviously substituted a baked loaf for the dough.

The costumes the actors wore were, on the whole, contemporary. Christianity to them was immediate, a part of their lives, not history. There was no attempt, as we do today, to think historically, and portray with visual accuracy or be careful about dates, fashions and 'period movement'. Even graphic and plastic artists did not try to portray men and women in the correct style and period of dress until well into the late sixteenth and early seventeenth centuries. The most an actor would use was a piece of drapery or a helmet to attempt 'antique dress' for Romans and Greeks, or a special dress for Eastern characters. No real sense of historical or geographical accuracy in theatre costume appears in England until the second half of the eighteenth century.

There were a few exceptions. Angels wore wings. The Magi wore crowns, had to resemble the three ages of man, and showed the country of their origin. God, too, was usually crowned. We hear of 'God in white leather with golden face and hair'. Devils wore animal masks and carried fireworks. They were hoofed, horned and tailed, clad in skins of rams, sheep, wolves and foxes. Upon their heads they wore the horns of cows, bulls, rams and deer. Bells hung about their waists and, as often as not, both buttocks and genitals represented, in grotesque form, a miniature 'Hell-Mouth'. Devils were portrayed both as male and female.

So the style of acting continued the ritualistic and formal presentation established by the Church, but by the late fourteenth century bawdy and very realistic performances are recorded intermingling with the sacred and mystical moments in the unfolding of the great epic. Performances were given even outdoing the extremist actors of the 'Method' school and Stanislavski in their desire for personal involvement. An actor who was playing Jesus 'would have died upon the rood-tree for he fainted and was like to have died, had he not been rescued'. A priest playing Judas 'hung too long and fainted and was like dead: for his heart failed him. Wherefore he was hastily taken down and carried to a place nearby and sprinkled with vinegar and other things to bring him to better'. Many actors playing Judas died hanging themselves. Some playing the part of Christ desired to undergo his sufferings, whilst others were badly burnt by fire.

Cycle plays were very ambitious, rich undertakings and few were given annually because of the tremendous cost, the organisation involved, the training of the actors and the regimentation of 'back-stage' assistants. Wagons, horses and their drivers, the makers of scenery, properties, masks, stage furniture and the costumes, mechanical devices and tricks, the re-writing and bringing up to date of the texts, all had to be considered. Some five hundred to well over a thousand men, women, and children, would have to be gathered together to make the performance of a large cycle-play possible.

The guilds had many duties including the payment of expenses to those taking part, feeding their actors during rehearsals, and fining those who were late or drunk! In Beverley a guild was fined a sum of money because it was considered that their actors were incompetent! Amongst items of guild expenditure which have survived in record books are:

> a pair of new gloves for Saint Thomas [Canterbury]
> a leather coat for Christ
> 5 prophets (one wanting) [Chelmsford, 1564]
> 3 skins for Noah's coat, making it and a rope to hang the ship in the
>   kirk . . . 7 shillings
> Thomas Sawyr to play God . . . 10d.
> a new pair of mittens for Noah . . . 4d. [Hull, 1494]
> a face and heare for y Father, A cote w hosen and tayle for ye serpents-
>   steyned [Norwich, 1565]
> linen cloths for the angels heads, and Jesus hoose
> Painting of angels wings . . . 8d. [Leicester, 1504]
> for Gabriel carrying a lily . . . 4d.

for playing God . . . 3 shillings
for a new coat and shoes for Gabriel . . . 35/4d.

This last expenditure, in relation to our present value of the pound, clearly indicates that a lot of money was spent in the making of fine and handsome costumes.

The organisation in getting each wagon to its appointed station, some having to play in as many as sixteen different areas of the town in a single day, and with well over thirty different plays to be performed, was a formidable task. The city would also have had to provide many 'traffic wardens'. To my knowledge we have no known reference to street-staffing, but a very interesting illustration from a French illuminated manuscript shows a man standing in the midst of a performance with a book in one hand and a wand of office in the other. Was he a general organiser, a prompter, a prologue, or did he take charge of the entire proceedings like a major-domo?

Of the four reasonably complete cycle texts surviving, the York cycle is perhaps the greatest and the most religious, with fifty-four independent plays making up the full cycle. They were all performed on the day of Corpus Christi, with between twelve and sixteen stations to move to. There was efficient supervision in the mounting and organisation, and the municipal authorities held a register containing a list of all the plays. Like Shakespeare's company of players, many actors were probably given more than one role to perform. It is considered that the cycle dates from the middle of the fourteenth century and we know that it was still being presented during the reign of Elizabeth I.

In the third year of Henry V's reign (1415), Roger Burton, then town clerk of York, compiled the following list and order of the plays:

*1. Tanners:*
God the father Almighty creating and forming the heavens.
*2. Plasterers:*
God the Father, in his substance, creating the earth.
*3. Cardmakers:*
God the Father creating Adam of the slime of the earth, and making Eve of the rib, and inspiring them with the spirit of life.
*4. Fullers* [= *cloth-cleaners*]:
God prohibiting Adam and Eve from eating of the tree of life.
*5. Coopers:*
Adam and Eve, tree betwixt them: serpent deceiving with apples.

6. *Armourers:*
Adam and Eve, an angel with a spade and a distaff assigning them labour.
7. *Gaunters* = [*glovers*]:
Abel and Cain killing sacrifices.
8. *Shipwrights:*
God foretelling Noah to make an ark of light wood.

> God: Thus thriftily and not over thin,
> Look that thy seams be subtly seen
> And nailed well, that they not twin:
> Thus I devised it should have been:
> Therefore do forth, and leave thy din.

After more instructions Noah commences to build:

> Noah: With nails that are both noble and new,
> Thus shall I fix it to the keel:
> Take here a rivet, and there a screw,
> With there bow, there now, work I well,
> This work, I warrant both good and true.

9. *Fishmongers, Pessyners [fishermen?], Mariners:*
Noah in the ark with his wife and three children and diverse animals.
10. *Perchemyners [= parchment-makers], Bookbinders:*
Abraham sacrificing his own son Isaac: a ram, a bush, and an angel.
11. *Hosiers:*
Moses exalting the serpent in the wilderness.
12. *Spicers:*
Mary and a doctor declaring the sayings of the prophets about the future birth of Christ: an angel saluting her.
13. *Pewterers, Founders:*
Mary, Joseph willing to put her away, an angel speaking to them that they should go to Bethlehem.
14. *Tylers:*
Mary, Joseph, a midwife, the child born lying in a manger betwixt an ox and an ass, and the angel speaking to the shepherds.
15. *Chandlers:*
The shepherds speaking by turns: the star in the east: an angel giving joy to the shepherds that a child was born.
16. *Goldsmiths, Orfeures [= watchmakers]:*
The three kings coming from the East.

17.  *Gold-beaters, Money-makers:*
Mary with the child and the star above, and the three kings offering gifts.
18.  *Masons:*
Mary with the child.
19.  *Marshals:*
Mary with the child, and Joseph flying into Egypt, by an angel's telling them.
20.  *Girdlers, Nailers, Sawters [ = psaltery-makers]:*
Herod commanding the children to be slain.
21.  *Sporiers [ = spur-makers], Lorymers [ = makers of small ironware]:*
The doctors, the child Jesus sitting in the temple in the midst of them, hearing them and asking them questions.
22.  *Barbers:*
Jesus, John the baptist baptising him, and two angels helping them.
23.  *Vintners:*
Jesus, Mary, bridegroom and bride.
24.  *Smiths, Fevers [ = metal-workers]:*
Jesus upon the pinnacle of the temple: Satan tempting with stones.
25.  *Corvisors [ = dressers of leather or shoemakers]:*
Peter, James and John: Jesus ascending into the mountain and trans-figuring himself before them.
26.  *Elennagers [ = examiners?]*
Simon the leper asking Jesus if he would eat with him. Two disciples: Mary Magdalene washing the feet of Jesus.
27.  *Plummers [ =dealers in plumes], Pattern-makers [ =mould-makers]:*
Jesus, two apostles, the woman taken in adultery, four Jews accusing her.
28.  *Pouch-makers, Botillers, Cap-makers:*
Lazarus in the sepulchre.
29.  *Vestment makers:*
Jesus upon an ass with its foal.
30.  *Cutlers, Blade-smiths, Sheathers, Scalers, Buckle-makers, Horners:*
Pilate, Caiaphas, two soldiers, three Jews, Judas selling Jesus.
31.  *Bakers, Water-leders [ = water-sellers]:*
The supper of the Lord and paschal Lamb, twelve apostles. The institution of the sacrament of the body of Christ in the new law, and communion of the Apostles.

32.  *Cordwainers* [= *shoemakers*] :
Pilate, Caiaphas, Annas, forty armed soldiers, Malchas, Peter, James, John, Jesus, and Judas kissing and betraying him.
33.  *Bowers* [= *bow-makers*], *Fletchers* [= *arrow-makers*] :
Striking and bastinadoing Christ.
34.  *Tapisers* [= *tapestry-makers*], *Couchers* [= *upholsterers*] :
Jesus, Pilate, Annas, Caiaphas: two counsellors and four Jews accusing Christ.
35.  *Littesters* [= *bed-makers*] :
Herod, two counsellors, four soldiers, Jesus, and three Jews.
36.  *Cukes* [= *cooks*], *Water-leders* :
Pilate, Annas, Caiaphas, two Jews, and Judas carrying with them thirty pieces of silver.
37.  *Sauce-makers* :
Judas hanging himself.
38.  *Milners* [= *milliners?*], *Tile-makers*, *Rope-makers*, *Cevers* [= *sewers or servers?*], *Turners*, *Hayresters* [= *Haymakers and hedgers*], *Bollers* [= *bowl- and pottery-makers*] :
Jesus, Pilate, Caiaphas, Annas, six soldiers carrying spears and ensigns, and another four leading Jesus from Herod desiring Barabbas to be released and Jesus to be crucified; three soldiers casting lots for the vesture of Jesus.
39.  *Shearmen* [= *wool-shearers*] :
Jesus covered with blood bearing his cross towards Mount Calvary.
40.  *Pynners* [= *pin-makers*], *Lateners* [= *makers of screens, doors, or perhaps lead-work for windows?*], *Painters* :
The cross, Jesus extended upon it on the earth: four Jews scourging him with whips, and afterwards erecting the cross.
41.  *Bouchers* [= *butchers*], *Pulterers* [= *poulterers*] :
The cross, two thieves crucified and Jesus suspended betwixt them.
42.  *Satellers* [= *saddlers*], *Sellers* [= *sellers of goods*], *Glaziers* :
Jesus destroying hell: twelve good and twelve evil spirits.
43.  *Carpenters, Joiners* :
The centurion declaring to Pilate, Caiaphas, and Annas, with other Jews, the signs appearing on the death of Jesus.
44.  *Cartwrights, Carvers, Sawyers* :
Jesus rising from the sepulchre.
45.  *Wyedrawers* [= *wire-drawers?*] :
Jesus, Mary, Mary Magdalene with spices.

46. *Broggers* [= *odd-jobbers*], *Wool-packers*, *Wadsmen* [= *binders or liners of clothes?*] :
Jesus, Luke and Cleophas in the form of travellers.
47. *Escriviners* [= *writers*], *Lumners* [= *illuminators*], *Questors* [= *pardoners*], *Dubbors* [= *renovators of old clothes*] :
John, James, Philip and other apostles: Thomas feeling the wounds of Jesus.
48. *Taillyoures* [= *tailors*] :
Mary, John the Evangelist, two angels, and eleven apostles: Jesus ascending before them, and four angels bearing a cloud.
49. *Potters* :
The Holy Ghost descending upon them, and four Jews admiring.
50. *Drapers* :
Jesus, Mary, Gabriel with two angels, two virgins and three Jews of the kindred of Mary, eight Apostles, and two devils.
51. *Lynwevers* [= *linen-weavers*] :
Four Apostles bearing the shrine of Mary.
52. *Wevers of Wollen* [= *wool-weavers*] :
Mary ascending with a multitude of angels.
53. *Hostilers* [= *innkeepers*] :
Mary, and Jesus crowning her with a great number of angels.
54. *Mercers* :
Jesus, Mary, twelve Apostles: four angels with trumpets, and four with a lance with two scourges: four good and four bad spirits, and six devils.

The Wakefield cycle (*c.* 1450) contains some thirty-two plays and was possibly adapted from a group of old York plays, though opinion is divided. The theme is a dramatic representation of man's salvation and it is assumed that it was written, or partly written, by one man, 'The Playwright of Wakefield'.

The most famous play, and read by many boys and girls at school in the study of English literature, is the *Second Shepherds' Play* or *Secunda Pastorum*. Its story is a parody on the theme of the birth of Christ. In it a Yorkshire countryman steals a sheep, and, to hide it, puts it in a cradle saying that his wife has just had a baby. When his plot is discovered he is tossed up into the air in a blanket for sheep-stealing. An angel sings and the scene changes to the Holy Land where shepherds take gifts to the Child—a ball, a bob of cherries and a bird.

Coventry's cycle (*c.* 1468) contains forty-three plays. Some evidence suggests that it was, at times, played on a permanent platform stage with a multiple setting of various mansions representing different scenes, and also that it may have been toured around from town to town by strolling players. Records of costumes and properties exist:

> A hanging curtain before the cross with a rope to draw it up.
> Gilding for the pillar and the cross.
> 2 pairs of gallows.
> A standard of red buckram.
> 4 gowns and 4 hoods for the Tormentors.
> 2 mitres for Caiaphas and Annas.
> God's coat of white leather needing six skins.
> 2 golden wigs for Jesus and Peter.

This is not a Corpus Christi play. The prologue states that the performance is given on a Sunday whereas the plays of Corpus Christi were always given on a Thursday. There are also hymns in the text.

Chester's cycle is considered by some to be the oldest, originally dating from the early part of the fourteenth century. It has twenty-five plays, and they contain country humour alongside religious instruction. Archdeacon Rogers, who saw the play in 1594, writes the following:

> The manner of these plays were, every company had his pageant ['pageant' comes from *pagina*, a board] . . . a high scaffold with two rooms, a higher and a lower, upon four wheels. In the lower they apparelled themselves, and in the higher room they played, being all open at the top, that all beholders might hear and see them. They began first at the abbey gates, and when the first pageant was played, it was wheeled to the high cross before the mayor, and so to every street. So every street had a pageant playing before it at one time, till all the pageants for the day appointed, were played. When one pageant was near ended, word was brought from street to street, that they might come in place thereof, exceedingly orderly, and all the streets have their pageants before them, all at one time playing together.

Plays in the Chester cycle include *The Fall of Lucifer, Abraham and Isaac, King Balack and Balaam with Moses, The Harrowing of the Resurrection, Whitsunday and the making of the Creed, Anti-Christ* and *Doomsday*.

Some of the ancient Welsh language is contained in the Cornish cycle. Early in origin, going back to 1300, and probably played on three separate days, being constructed in three parts—'The Origin of the World', 'The Passion of Christ', and 'The Resurrection of Christ'—it includes themes on the legend of the Holy Rood and the Oil of Mercy. The text (some fifty episodes) contains five circular plans showing the staging of the plays, with detailed stage directions for presentation 'in the round'—the old pagan ritual areas, like the one at St Just in Cornwall, no doubt were used and adapted regularly for the performances. This play, we know, was still being performed well into the years of Elizabeth's reign. A survey of Cornwall by Richard Carew published in 1602 includes the following:

> A miracle play, is a kind of interlude, compiled in Cornish out of some Scripture History with that grossness which accompanied the Romanes vetus Comedia. For representing it, they raise an earthen amphitheatre in some field having the diameter of this enclosed plain some 40 or 50 feet. The Country people flock from all sides, many miles off to hear and see it; for they have therein devils and devices, to delight as well the eye as the ear; the players con their parts without book, but are prompted by one called the Ordinary, who followeth at their back with the book in his hand, and telleth them softly what they must pronounce aloud.

The day, or days, of a performance of a cycle play were public holidays. These holidays brought hundreds of visitors to the town from the villages and outlying districts. Shakespeare, as a youth, must have visited Coventry to see their plays, and much of his early work (and most other Elizabethan dramatists as well) shows a direct influence, particularly the scheme of writing one short scene after another. Shakespeare's plays, in particular the chronicles, echo in their constant change of scene, or scene division, this epic style in many scenes to make the whole. *Henry VI* has 27 scenes in Part 1; 24 scenes in Part 2; and 28 scenes in Part 3. *Antony and Cleopatra* shows some 42 scene divisions, with many of the scenes occupying no more than a half dozen lines or so. Marlowe's two-part epic *Tamburlaine*, written between 1587 and 1588, is divided into 18 scenes for Part 1 and 21 scenes for Part 2. The descriptions of the entrances of the characters and the stage furniture required shows a close affinity to the style and presentation of the miracle and mystery plays.

> To the battle and Mycetes comes out alone with his crown in his hand, offering to hide it.
> Tamburlaine goes to her, and takes her away lovingly by the hand, looking wrathfully on Agydas and says nothing.

Enter two Moors drawing Bajazeth in his cage, his wife following him.

The banquet, and to it cometh Tamburlaine all in scarlet.

Enter four Virgins with branches of laurel in their hands.

Enter Tamburlaine all in black and very melancholy.

He brains himself against the cage.

The arras is drawn, and Zenocrate lies in her bed of state; Tamburlaine sitting by her; three Physicians about her bed, tempering potions.

The music sounds and she dies.

Drums, sounding a doleful march; the town burning.

Tamburlaine, drawn in his chariot by Trebizon and Soria, with bits in their mouths, reins in his left hand, and in his right hand a whip with which he scourgeth them; Techelles, Theridamas, Usumcasane, Amyras, Celebinus, Natolia and Jerusalem, led by five or six common Soldiers.

Enter the Governor of Babylon upon the walls with others.

Enter with others; two spare kings.

While the young Elizabethan playwrights were writing for their public playhouses and the Court down in London, the folk in the Midlands were still enjoying their great festival days, the performances of their cycles, and the dramatic representation of their faith. But they could not last much longer, for all religious dogma was under pressure and constant change. It was foolhardy to present these plays when there was the constant fear of an accusation of heresy and the punishment of torture and death. All religious dramas and age-old customs were either altered or censored, or banned. Episodes directly referring to or depicting the Virgin, the Sacrament, the saints, and later God himself, had to go.

There was also competition from the professional actors who were by now regularly playing their morality plays and their interludes with less, and sometimes no, direct reference to the Bible at all. Professional playwrights included songs, mimes and dances. School and college mentors were busily writing their own plays based upon Italianate classical scholarship. These plays offered a greater freedom for thought and perhaps an escape from the bloody battle of religious politics.

The world was changing fast to accept a new concept of man, who had to identify himself and adapt his way of life to new thoughts and new beliefs, rather than to accept his existence as part of the old accepted structure of divine guidance and order.

The mysteries could not be understood through reason and logic alone.

The churchyard and west façade, Winchester Cathedral

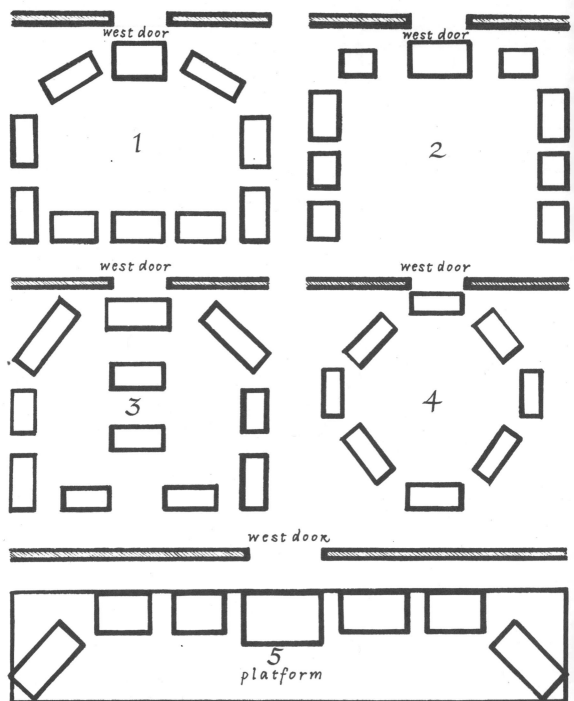

west door

1

west door

2

west door

3

4

west door

west door

5

platform

5 METHODS OF ARRANGING THE MANSIONS, OR STAGES, IN FRONT OF THE WEST DOOR OF THE CHURCH and/or IN THE TOWN SQUARE:

1 Four Sided  2 Three Sided  3 Around & About  4 Circular  5 Running Across the front of the Church on a Platform to resemble a Street

strangling

the stocks

hanging

beheading by sword

whipping

beheading by the axe

Some Public Spectacles

A Mediaeval Walled City

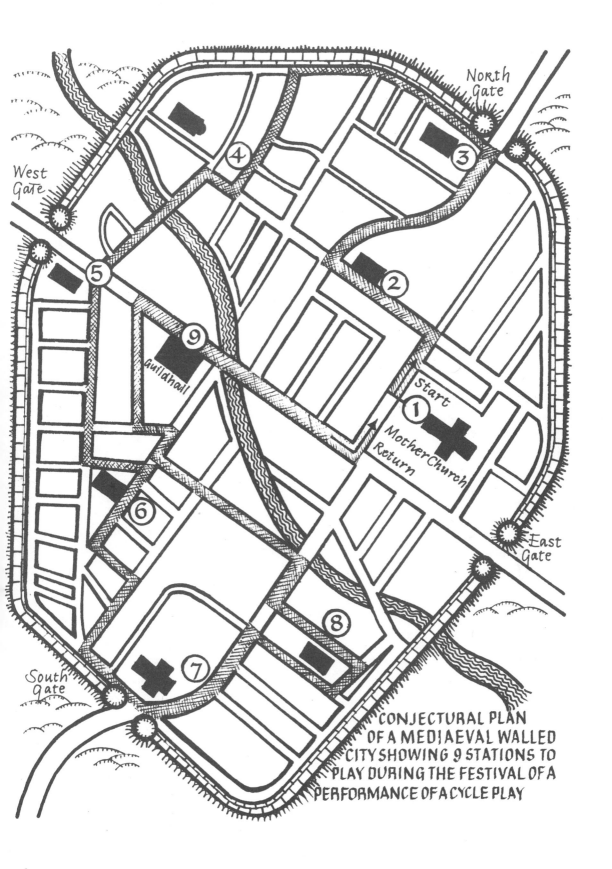

North Gate

West Gate

East Gate

South Gate

Start
Mother Church
Return

Guildhall

④ ③ ② ⑤ ⑨ ① ⑥ ⑧ ⑦

CONJECTURAL PLAN OF A MEDIAEVAL WALLED CITY SHOWING 9 STATIONS TO PLAY DURING THE FESTIVAL OF A PERFORMANCE OF A CYCLE PLAY

The Golden Horn

The Sun

The Castle

The Three Bells

The Golden Fleece

INN SIGNS

The Crossed Keys

A Mediaeval Representation of Noah's Ark

A Wagon Stage Presentation of
'Noah & the Flood'
(conjectural)

Pageant Wagon presenting the Story of Adam & Eve
Using both the upper and lower acting areas

The Hell Pageant

conjectural

# Noah's Ark

*conjectural*

# Pageant Wagon of the Crucifixion

The Pageant of the Last Supper

The Feeding of the Five Thousand

conjectural

The Wedding at Cana

The Pageant of the Raising of Lazarus

A Page of Devils and a Prompter

All based on manuscript drawings or stone carvings

Based on a Manuscript drawing in the BM

Hell's Mouth

CF

England

Carlisle
Durham
Kendal
Lancaster
Halifax York Beverley
Wakefield Hull
Lincoln
Chester Nottingham
Derby
Shrewsbury Leicester Norwich
Coventry Ely Yarmouth
Cambridge Lavenham
Ludlow
Worcester Stratford Bedford Colchester
Gloucester Oxford St. Albans
Bristol Windsor London
Bath Eton
Wells Canterbury
Glastonbury Salisbury Dover
Southamp'on Chichester Hastings Rye
Exeter Bodiam

SOME IMPORTANT
TOWNS IN THE
LATE MIDDLE
AGES

114

# 4

# In the Schools, in the Home, and in the Streets

## *Instruction versus Entertainment*

Professional actors had appeared in morality plays and interludes since the fourteenth century, touring the towns where mystery cycles were given. Whereas the mystery plays were simply naive dramatisations of the Bible, the morality plays were a more intellectual entertainment involving a dramatised argument and requiring the audience to take sides with 'the good' or 'the bad'. It is not surprising that they came to be used as instruction in schools and universities in the late fifteenth and sixteenth centuries and that, as the old blinded religious beliefs began to crumble, their subjects moved away from the Bible into the field of allegory and concentrated on 'rules for the conduct of life'. Many were written as celebrations of victory as in the instance of the performance of a moral play for Henry V when he returned from Agincourt in 1415 and again when he returned to England with his French bride.

When scholars took over the morality plays, the man in the street was left behind . . . and so were many of the travelling actors who cut their plays to 'interludes' and put in more comedy and bawdy lines to keep their popular appeal.

In early morality plays, the Seven Deadly Sins were basic characters (Pride, Lust, Sloth, Gluttony, Hatred, Avarice and Anger) and the only comic relief was provided by the Devil, accompanied by his 'Vice' or buffoon. Apart from the 'instructional' moralities based on an episode in the Bible, there were 'Dialogue' moralities, 'Death' moralities, and 'Struggle' moralities about the fight between a virtue and a vice for the human soul.

The 'Dialogue' morality, very popular in Anglo-Saxon England, was a wordy mock battle of disputation such as medieval clerics had fought but between two actors, playing characters such as Death versus Life, Wine arguing it out with Water, or Winter with Summer. In *c.* 1400 appears *The Cuckoo and the Nightingale* and even earlier *The Owl and the Nightingale,* with the owl standing for a gravity of purpose whilst the nightingale argues for beauty, sweetness and joy (a typical conflict between age and youth). Shakespeare makes reference to, and uses, this antique form in *Love's Labours Lost* :

> But, most esteemed greatness, will you hear the dialogue that the two learned men have compiled in praise of the owl and the cuckoo? It should have followed in the end of our show. . . . This side is *Hiems*, Winter: this *Ver*, the Spring: the one maintained by the owl, th'other by the cuckoo. *Ver*, begin. [Armado: Act V, Scene 2.]

and his *Troilus and Cressida* is arguably the most elaborate and sophisticated example of the 'dialogue' morality, using as its theme the importance of unity and the stupidity of war.

'Death' moralities such as *Everyman* (by definition not old or young, rich or poor, healthy or ill) opened up the possibility for real characterisation, as opposed to two-dimensional writing, of people neither entirely good nor entirely bad. A dramatic struggle exists and a psychological understanding of man is evident. Everyman moves forward, gets frightened and is reluctant to face himself. He begins to find courage, then fails, until in the end (after many conflicts) he meets, with joy and understanding, death, entering his grave ready to stand before his God. Simple 'picture-book' characters thus disappeared to give place to complex psychological issues which only man himself can decide . . . such as how to come to terms with death. England's version of *Everyman* does not appear until the early part of the sixteenth century and was probably taken from a Dutch play which in turn may have been derived from an old Buddhist parable. It is the most famous and beautiful play of its kind and is still regularly performed in England and on the Continent, particularly Germany.

'Struggle' moralities include *All for Money* or *Money is the root of all Evil* or the *Morality of Welth and Helth*, requiring four actors 'very merry and full of pastyme'. The last and most ambitious of the 'Struggle' moralities was Marlowe's *Doctor Faustus* (*c.* 1590). The theme is a conflict on the outcome of selling one's soul to the devil. Many of the characters are taken direct from the old religious plays: Lucifer, Prince of Hell; Beelzebub; Mephistopheles, one-time servant of Beelzebub; a Good and an Evil Angel; and the Seven Deadly Sins. Faust travels the world on a dragon, male and female devils constantly appear, tricks are played on the Pope, fireworks explode, Faustus loses his leg, characters are turned into an ape and a dog, and the spirits of Alexander the Great and Helen of Troy make an appearance. His complexity of many scenes and stage characters, both serious and comic, requires very elaborate devices and costumes for performance.

In the earlier 'moral' plays 'Knowledge' was possibly presented as a splendid woman—her dress decorated with eyes, ears and mouths, and an actor representing 'Grammar' probably carried a knife ready to attack students' errors. One of the morality plays *The Castle of Perseverance* copies the circular staging of the old Cornish cycles. A plan from an existent text shows the method of presentation very clearly—including production notes and the dressing of the actors:

> Belyal the devil must have burning gun-powder in pipes in his hands, ears, and arse when he goes into battle. The four daughters Mercy, Peace, Truth and Righteousness wear mantles; Mercy—white, Peace—black, Truth—sad green and Righteousness—red.
> Stewards must control the crowds who are to be separated from the action by a ditch (some favoured guests *may* be allowed in the 'place' or playing area).

Interludes were based upon an argument involving two or more characters who were sometimes disguised. The plays were, more often than not, short and written for a small group of players—four men and two boys who played the women's parts. Interludes can be divided into five categories:

1  *Moral.* A fight between a vice and a virtue for the possession of a man's soul, a shortened form of the 'Struggle' morality.
2  *Political.*
3  *Pedagogical.* One such play, *The Marriage of Wit and Science*, written during the earlier part of the sixteenth century by John Redford, master of the singing boys at Saint Paul's, uses songs and dances, including the galliard. Requiring very little in the way of scenery, the characters are 'Wit', a student who wins his girlfriend 'Science' in marriage; 'Reason' is the name given to her father.
4  *Historical.* These were very popular but few remain. Dramatising the lives and deeds of English kings, the action is fast and epic with a constantly shifting plot and change of scene. Shakespeare and Marlowe were no doubt influenced by this early form when they began to write their own great histories and chronicles. John Bale (1495–1563), Bishop of Ossory, and sometimes known as Billious Bale, on his own evidence

wrote more than twenty plays including a large miracle play (now lost) and others of a religious nature strongly attacking popery and priests. His *King Johan* not only includes real characters, but also characters in the abstract like 'Private Wealth' (Cardinal Pandulph?), 'Dissimulation' and 'England'. Similarly, Shakespeare has 'Rumour, the Presenter' in *Henry IV*, Part 2, enter 'painted full of tongues'.

5 *Comic*. John Heywood (1497–1580) leaves us with six. Another master of the boys of Saint Paul's, his plays were written to be performed at Court, most likely by his pupils. In *The Play of the Weather* various messengers ask Jupiter (as God was vicariously called) for the weather most favourable to their work: in the end Jupiter delivers his judgement . . . that the English weather shall remain changeable It contains songs, and was staged so that actors could move through the audience. A throne is needed for Jupiter, 'capable of concealment', and also torches, either to represent night symbolically, or for evening performances. *The Four P's*, set 'somewhere on an English road', is farcical and close in style to a Dialogue morality. Taking place 'once upon a time', it concerns four characters, the Pardoner, the Pothecary, the Palmer and the Pedlar, competing to see who can tell the biggest lie, with the last lines reading:

'To pass the time in this without offense
Was the cause why the maker did make it.'

By 1550 it is hard to differentiate between the interlude and the new plays, save for their length. There was little emphasis on morality, though the subject was often serious. When performed at Court or during banquets, emphasis was not only on instruction, but also on entertainment and visual delight, pointing the way to the masque. The earliest interlude not to include the Devil as a character is *Nature* by Henry Medwell, chaplain to the household of Cardinal John Morton, Archbishop of Canterbury at the time of King Henry VII. Divided into two parts, it appears to have been written as a Christmas interlude in 1497 to be played during the courses at a banquet when the Archbishop was entertaining ambassadors from Spain and Flanders. It was based on a Roman theme, *De Vera Nobilitate*, translated by the Earl of Worcester and printed by William Caxton (1442–1491), about the qualities needed to make a gentleman. Besides the serious argument, Medwell includes a secondary comic plot involving a maid and two servants, a dual situation which was enjoyed so much later on by Elizabethan audiences. Medwell also wrote *Fulgens and Lucrece*, a play requiring a small cast of only seven characters, whereas *Nature* has twenty-two.

The Master of the Revels at Court, first documented in 1494, supervised and paid for the interludes at royal banquets, marriages, birthdays and other important celebrations. These were usually played by small professional companies, the most used being 'The Players of the King's Interlude' *(Lusores Regis)* who were performing for Henry VII in 1493. This company had half a dozen men, later to increase in number, who were paid a retainer and extra monies when called upon to give entertainments. They attended the wedding celebrations of Princess Margaret and James IV in Scotland and are last heard of during the reign of Elizabeth I.

In the formative years of the sixteenth century, considerable numbers of companies of players arose under the protection of the Court or some wealthy nobleman, who may also have fancied himself as an actor. Even the redoubtable young Thomas More would 'slip in among the players' and improvise his own performance. Unless players were licensed, or under the protection of some great household, they were still considered 'rogues and vagabonds' and were liable to severe punishments and penalties, a ruling to continue throughout the reigns of both Elizabeth I and James I and to become even more wretchedly severe during the Commonwealth. Strolling players, however, continued with their interludes well into the seventeenth century, as a writer recalls in 1639:

> In the city of Gloucester, the manner is (as I think it is in other corporations) that when players of interludes come to the town they first attend the mayor, to inform him what nobleman's servant they are, and so to get licence for their public playing; and if the mayor like the actors, or would shew respect to their lord and master, he appoint them to play their first play before himself and the aldermen and common council of the city; and that is called the mayor's play, where everyone that will, comes in without money, the mayor giving the players a reward as he thinks fit to shew respect unto them. At such a play my father took me with him, and made me stand between his legs, as he sat upon one of the benches, where we saw and heard very well.

The staging was basically simple—a raised platform with steps leading up from the audience, a curtained background, and only the absolute essentials in the way of good properties, as fine a set of costumes as they could acquire, and simple scenery. Itinerant actors relied for their success on the vigour of their playing and on audience participation—some interludes had songs for the audience to join in. When they risked playing without a licence, a collection of money or food was taken at the end.

So professional drama was established and the way was open for the great Elizabethan plays. There is another area, outside the moralities and interludes, to be surveyed: the amateur influence of the classically-minded schoolmasters, tutors and lawyers. The choirboy interludes were not the only form of drama in the grammar school curriculum; every young gentleman was expected to read Latin plays; university undergraduates both read and played in Latin and English; and lawyers in the Inns of Court did not restrict their histrionic talents to appearing before magistrates. *Ralph Roister Doister* is one of the earliest examples of a school play influenced by acquaintance with classical drama (Roman, not Greek, since the boys were fed on Terence, Plautus, and Seneca). Their diet began with classical masterpieces played before their fellow pupils and invited guests, then to a course of 'home-produce', usually written by one of the masters and based on the theories of Italian scholarship—play structure, staging, and the 'unities' set out by Aristotle, demanding control over the time element, the place and the action. *Ralph Roister Doister* is set in a village street, the unities are reasonably adhered to, but the atmosphere is English in spirit and not Roman. Adapted from *Miles Gloriosus* by Plautus, it was the 'home-production' of Nicholas Udall (1505–1556), a master at Eton. It is in five acts and contains songs, with the stage setting planned in the manner of Serlio. Serlio (1475–1554) was an Italian painter, architect, and innovator of new concepts in the designing of theatrical buildings, stage scenery, and in particular the art of perspectives. He based his conclusions on the concepts of the Ancients, particularly Marcus Vitruvius Pollio, a Roman architect and engineer working under Augustus, who was in turn influenced by Greek thought in the methods of staging plays. The three basic classical stage settings were for comedy, a street with doors and windows and balconies to the several buildings; for tragedy, a lofty temple or palace or town square, with vertical composition to emphasise dignity, and for a satyric play a wood, glade or grotto. *Ralph Roister Doister*, being a comedy, was probably presented with the house of Roister on one side of the stage and Dame Custance's house on the other, a backcloth representing a continuation of the street, with space between the two houses allowing for a central entrance. Most of the action would have been played in the central area so as not to destroy the illusion of the perspective!

*Gammer Gurton's Needle*, written at about the same time and probably acted by scholars at Christ's College, Cambridge, requires much the same kind of setting—a village street with Dame Gurton's house on one side and Dame Chat's on the other. This play, like most, is in rhymed couplets, with music and songs including 'Backe and syde go bare, go bare'.

As for the lawyers, Seneca influenced Sackville and Norton when they wrote *Gorboduc*, the first English tragedy in blank verse rather than the fashionable rhymed doggerel, for the gentlemen of the Inner Temple to play before Elizabeth in 1557. Based upon legendary English 'history', the theme is on the rightful succession to the crown. Queen Elizabeth had been monarch just four years, and there were still rivals to the throne!

*Gorboduc* combines both Senecan and medieval concepts in presentation. Seneca wanted his plays recited and not acted. Medieval drama regularly separated movement from language, and mime from rhetoric. Was the playwright not yet skilful enough to combine action with words? The play is in five acts. Every act is preceded by a dumb show to point the moral, and each act has, as its conclusion, a chorus or narrator. The five dumb shows, including instruction on what musical instruments should accompany them, are so important in visual description that they should be read in full:

Act I; First the music of violins began to play, during which came in upon the stage six wild men, clothed in leaves. Of whom the first bare in his neck a fagot of small sticks, which they all, both severally and together, assayed with all their strength to break, but it could not be broken by them. At the length one of them plucked out one of the sticks and brake it: and the rest plucking out all the other sticks one after another did easily break them, the same being severed, which being conjoined they had before attempted in vain. After they had this done, they departed the stage, and the music ceased. Hereby was signified, that a state knit in unity doth continue strong against all force, but being divided, is easily destroyed: as befell upon Duke Gorboduc dividing his land to his two sons, which he before held in monarchy; and upon the dissention of the brethren, to whom it was divided.

. . .

Act II: First the music of cornets began to play, during which came in upon the stage a king accompanied with a number of his nobility and gentlemen. And after he had placed himself in a chair of estate prepared for him, there came and kneeled before him a grave and aged gentleman, and offered up a cup unto him of wine in a glass, which the king refused. After him comes a brave and lusty young gentleman, and presents the king with a cup of gold filled with poison, which the king accepted, and drinking the same, immediately fell down dead upon the stage, and so was carried thence away by his lords and gentlemen, and then the music ceased. Hereby was signified, that as a glass by nature holdeth no poison, but is clear and may easily be seen through, he boweth by any art; so a faithful counsellor holdeth no treason, but is plain and open, ne yeildeth to any undiscreet affection, but giveth wholesome counsel, which the ill-advised prince refuseth. The delightful gold filled with poison betokeneth flattery, which under fair seeming of pleasant words beareth deadly poison, which destroyed the prince that receiveth it. As befel in the two brethren, Ferrex and Porrex, who, refusing the wholesome advice of grave counsellors, credited these young parasites, and brought to themselves death and destruction thereby.

· · ·

Act III: First the music of flutes began to play, during which came in upon the stage a company of mourners all clad in black, betokening death and sorrow to ensue upon the ill-advised misgovernment and dissention of brethren, as befell upon the murder of Ferrez by his younger brother. After the mourners had passed thrice about the stage, they departed, and then the music ceased.

· · ·

Act IV: First the music of hautboys began to play, during which there came forth from under the stage, as though out of hell, three furies, Alecto, Megaera, and Tisiphone, clad in black garments sprinkled with blood and flames, their bodies girt with snakes, their heads spread with serpents instead of hair, the one bearing in her hand a snake, the other a whip, and the third a burning firebrand: each driving before them a king and queen which, moved by the furies, unnaturally had slain their own children. The names of the kings and queens were these: Tantalus, Medea, Athamas, Ino, Cambyses, Althea. After that the furies and these had passed about the stage thrice, they departed, and then the music ceased. Hereby was signified the unnatural murders to follow, that is to say: Porrex slain by his own mother, and of king Gorboduc and queen Viden, killed by their own subjects.

· · ·

Act V: First the drums and the flutes began to sound, during which there came forth upon the stage a company of arquebusiers, and of armed men, all in order of battle. These, after their pieces discharged, and that the armed men had three times marched about the stage, departed, and then the drums and flutes did cease. Hereby was signified tumults, rebellions, arms, and civil wars to follow, as fell in the realm of Great Britain, which, by the space of fifty years and more, continued in civil war between the nobility after the death of king Gorboduc and of his issues, for want of certain limitation in succession of the crown, till the time of Dunwallo Molmutius, who reduced the land to monarchy.

This play bridges the gap between the formal and symbolic style of church drama and the more realistic style of writing and presentation during the reign of Elizabeth I. Shakespeare, in *Hamlet* Act III, Scene 2, reminds his audience of this antique form when the strolling players entertain Claudius and his court—a dumb show followed by the same story relying almost entirely on the rhymed spoken word.

The trumpets sound. The Dumb-show follows; Enter a King and Queen very lovingly. The Queen embraces him, and he her. She kneels and makes show of protestation unto him. He takes her up and declines his head upon her neck. He lays down upon a bank of flowers. She leaves him seeing him asleep. Anon comes in another man, who taking off his crown kisses it, pours poison into the sleeper's ears, and leaves. The Queen returns, finds the King dead and makes passionate action. The Poisoner, with some three or four, comes in again, seeming to condole her. The dead body is carried away. The Poisoner wooes the Queen with gifts: she seems harsh and unwilling, but in the end accepts his love.

Playwrights were often heavily criticised. Sir Philip Sydney (an unsuccessful playwright) in his 'An Apologie for Poetrie' writes in 1581:

Our tragedies and comedies (not without cause cried out against), observing rules neither of honest civility nor of skillful poetry, excepting *Gorboduc* (again, I say, of those that I have seen), which, notwithstanding as it is full of stately speeches and well-sounding phrases, climbing to the height of Seneca in style, and as full of notable morality, which it doth most delightfull teach, and so obtain the very end of poesy, yet in troth it is very defectious in the circumstances; which grieveth me, because it might not remain as an exact model of all tragedies. For it is faulty both in place and time, the two necessary companions of all corporal actions. For where the stage should always represent but one place, and the uttermost time presupposed in it should be, both by Aristotle's precept

123

and common reason, but one day, there is both many days and many places, inartificially imagined. But if it be so in *Gorboduc*, how much more in all the rest? where you shall have Asia of the one side, and Afric of the other, and so many other, underkingdomes, that the player, when he cometh in, must ever begin with telling where he is: or else, the tale will not be conceived. Now ye shall have three ladies walk to gather flowers, and then we must believe the stage to be a garden. By and by, we hear news of a shipwreck in the same place, and then we are to blame, if we accept it not for a rock. Upon the back of that, comes out a hideous monster with fire and smoke, and then the miserable beholders are bound to take it for a cave. While in the meantime two armies fly in, represented with four swords and bucklers, and then what hard heart will not receive it for a pitched field? Now of time they are much more liberal, for ordinary it is that two young princes fall in love. After many traverses, she is got with child, delivered of a fair boy, he is lost, groweth a man, falls in love, and is ready to get another child: and all this in two hours' space: which how absurd it is in sense, even sense may imagine, . . . But besides these gross absurdities, how all their plays be neither right tragedies nor right comedies: mingling kings and clowns, not because the matter so carrieth it, but thrust in clowns by head and shoulders, to play a part in majestical matters, with neither decency nor discretion. So as neither the admiration and commiseration nor the right sportful- ness is by their mongrel tragi-comedy obtained.

The average Englishman, however, enjoyed a mixture of plots, styles, many scenes, tragic and comic characters intermingling with one another— prince and pauper together—and he liked his imagination to be stimulated. His taste was formed by the old church and street plays which were his heritage.

*The Lamentable Tragedy, Mixed Full of Pleasant Mirth, Containing The Life of Cambises, King of Persia* (*c.* 1558–1570) was his 'cup of tea'. It shows a strong influence from the old morality play and the historical tragedy, with abstract characters explaining much of the action, which is contrived by 'Ambidexter', the Vice. A mixture of horror, farce, history and allegory, it was possibly written for a professional group of touring actors—six men and two boys. Very little is required in the way of scenery and stage properties, and it could easily have been performed on a trestled platform with just a couple of entrances or exits. The title page shows the division of parts:

| | | | |
|---|---|---|---|
| Councell | | Cambises | |
| Huff | | Epilogue | For one man |
| Praxaspes | For one man | | |
| Murder | | Prologue | |
| Lob | | Sisamnes | |
| The Third Lord | | Diligence | |
| | | Cruelties | For one man |
| Lord | | Hob | |
| Ruf | | Preparation | |
| Common Cry | | The I Lord | |
| Commons Complaint | For one man | | |
| Lord Smirdis | | Ambidexter | |
| Venus | | Triall | For one man |
| Knight | | Menatrix | |
| Snuf | | Shame | |
| Small Hability | | Otian | |
| Proof | For one man | Mother | For one man |
| Execution | | Lady | |
| Attendance | | Queen | |
| Second Lord | | | |

Young child
Cupid } For one man

For the strolling players of this kind of play, their theatres were mostly inn yards. We know that the following London inns were used for stage performances until the Great Plague in the 1590s:

> The Red Lion, Stepney
> The Cross Keys Inn, Gracechurch Street
> The Bull Inn, Bishopsgate Street
> The Boars Head Inn, Aldgate
> The Bel Savage Inn, Ludgate Hill
> The Bell Inn, Gracechurch Street.

In and out of London, the yard of an inn had many advantages. There was a ready-made audience drawn from the guests occupying rooms and also, being well situated in a busy part of the town, from the local citizens, merchants, workers and apprentices. Architecturally, the inn yard was a square open courtyard with rooms, stores and stables running around on all four sides. Piercing one or sometimes two of the sides was a large arch to permit the entrance of a horse, or on very rare occasions, a coach. This great arch was closed by heavy doors, which contained a smaller door for the use of late arrivals at the inn at night. The smaller door, with a wicket or spy hole, was very useful during a performance of a play to regulate the flow of the audience, to give some measure of control in taking entrance money and to keep out undesirables such as thugs, people suspect of the plague, cut-purses, and the local whores (who, although some might bring business with them, mostly waited for customers arriving to see the play and then took them off.)

Stephen Gosson in his *The Schoole of Abuses* (1579) complains:

In our assemblies at plays in London, you shall see such heaving, and shoving, such itching and shouldering to sit by women: such care for their garments, that they be not trod on: such eyes to their laps, that no chips [ideas] light in them: such pillows to their backs, that they take no hurt: such masking in their ears, I know not what: such giving them pip-pens to pass the time: such playing at footsaunt ['footsie-footsie'] without cards: such tickling, such toying, such smiling, such winking, and such manning their home [escorting them and then pressing their advantage!], when the sports are ended, that it is a right comedy to mark their be-haviour, to watch their conceits, as the cat for the mouse, and as good as a course at the game itself, to dog them a little, or follow aloof by the print of feet, and so discover by slot where the deer taketh soil. If this were as well noted as seen, or as openly punished as secretly practised, I have no doubt but the cause would be seared to dry up the effect, and these pretty rabbits very cunningly ferreted from their burrows. For they that lack customers all the week, either because their haunt is unknown or the constables and officers of their parish watch them so narrowly that they dare not quetch [utter a sound], to celebrate the sabbath flock to theatres, and there keep a general market of bawdry. Not that any filthiness in deed is committed within the compass of that ground, as was done in Rome, but that every wanton and his paramour, every man and his mistress, every John and his Joan, every knave and his quean, are there first aquainted and cheapen the merchandise in that place, which they pay for elsewhere as they can agree.

A letter from the Lord Mayor and Aldermen of the City of London to the Privy Council as late as 1597 shows that things had not improved:

1. They [the plays] are a special cause of corrupting youth, containing nothing but unchaste matters, lascivious devices, shifts of cozenage, and other lewd and ungodly practises, being so as that they impress the very quality and corruption of manners which they represent, contrary to the rules and art prescribed for the making of comedies even among the heathen, who used them seldom and at certain set times, and not all the year long as our manner is. Whereby such as frequent them, being of the base and refuse sort of people or such young gentlemen as have small regard of credit or conscience, draw the same into imitation and not to the avoiding the like vices which they represent.

2. They are the ordinary places for vagrant persons, masterless men, thieves, horse-stealers, whoremongers, cozeners, coney-catchers, contrivers of treason and other idle and dangerous persons to meet together and to make their matches to the great displeasure of Almighty God and the hurt and annoyance of her Majesty's people: which cannot be prevented nor discovered by the governers of the city for that they are out of the city's jurisdiction.

3. They maintain idleness in such persons as have no vocation, and draw apprentices and other servants from their ordinary works and all sorts of people from the resort unto sermons and other Christian exercises to the great hindrance of trades and profanation of religion established by her Highness within this realm.

4. In the time of sickness is to be found by experience that many, having sores and yet not heart-sick, take occasion hereby to walk abroad and to recreate themselves by hearing a play. Whereby others are infected, and themselves also many things miscarry.

So the actors were blamed both for taking people from church on a Sunday *and* for spreading the plague!

At the start of the play, guests at the inn came on to the balconies with their stools, chairs, benches and cushions, or simply stood to watch the performance from above, whilst the 'outside' audience stood tightly packed in the yard below. A trestled stage would be set in front of one of the inn's great arches in which was hung a painted cloth or curtains as a permanent background to the play. The curtain may have been divided down the middle to allow for a surprise central entrance, and even to open revealing a throne, a bed or another room, but most of the entrances came through the audience, as with the interludes. The actors used the rooms closest to the stage as dressing and retiring rooms, moving from these rooms and through the audience, already establishing the character they were playing, up a small flight of steps on to the stage to make an entrance. The procedure would be reversed for an exit. (This method of playing can still be seen today in southern Europe, where travelling companies regularly 'use' their audience because of temporary staging.) Noisy and vigorous audiences, including the village louts, no doubt 'sent up' the show, but got good return for their money from the actors' ability to improvise and to use their wits!

Stage furniture was kept to a minimum. Only pieces essential to describe the action of the scene were used, as it was too difficult and clumsy to remove furniture from the stage other than by pulling back the curtain to conceal it, get rid of it, or replace it, so they travelled with a couple of thrones, a bed, a bench or two, and a painted tree or bush. But what they lacked in furniture they made up for in the spectacle of dress, and the properties which could be easily carried on and off the stage by the actors with complete naturalness: banners and shields, canopies, litters, swords, pikes and lighted torches (to represent night). Dressed in crowns and robes of state, tabards and armour, and highly elaborate dresses for fantastical characters, costuming was the chief expense in its rich and visual display.

The actor's skill was a combination of rhetoric, verse and prose, mime and symbolic gesturing, and dance, with at times earthy naturalistic interpretations and improvisation based upon 'ordinary' or country people. They were cunning and skilful in their stage management and with their use of sound, music, and song. Elizabethan drama was thus directly linked to the old detached scenes played in church, the great pageant plays of the guilds, the moralities and the interludes, with some of the new-fangled eloquence in Italianate staging and the style and art of argument and debate encouraged in school and college education.

The stage had been set for Christopher Marlowe and William Shakespeare.

Reconstruction of the Opening Scene in Everyman c1480

ABSTRACT CHARACTERS
FROM MORALITY PLAYS

Idolatry

ape

Philosophy

clouds

book

pen

ladder

Luxury

mirror

sceptre

spear

throne

Prudence

serpent

Adapted from Stained Glass c1360-1400

130

*from a manuscript in the BM*

Scenes of Instruction

Beware of Money & Evil Thoughts

131

14th ALLEGORICAL CHARACTER representing SUN

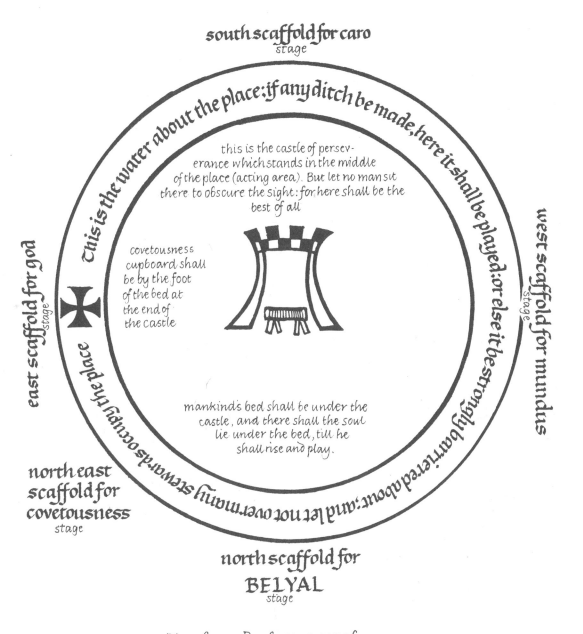

south scaffold for caro
stage

This is the water about the place: if any ditch be made, here it shall be played: or else it be strongly barriered about; and let not overmany stewards occupy the place

this is the castle of perseverance which stands in the middle of the place (acting area). But let no man sit there to obscure the sight: for here shall be the best of all

covetousness cupboard shall be by the foot of the bed at the end of the castle

mankind's bed shall be under the castle, and there shall the soul lie under the bed, till he shall rise and play.

west scaffold for mundus
stage

east scaffold for god
stage

north east
scaffold for
covetousness
stage

north scaffold for
BELYAL
stage

Plan for a Performance of

THE CASTLE OF PERSEVERANCE
c 1425

133

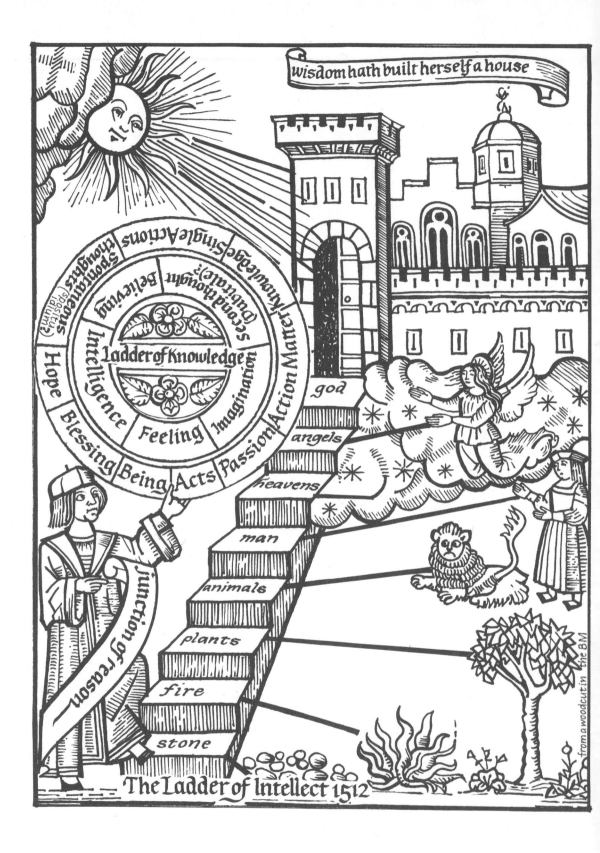

The Ladder of Intellect 1512

wisdom hath built herself a house

Ladder of Knowledge

Spontaneous (speaks natural?) Thoughts · Single Actions · many Actions · Matter · Action · Passion · Imagination · Feeling · Intelligence · Hope · Blessing · Being · Acts · second thought (Dubitale?) · Believing

god · angels · heavens · man · animals · plants · fire · stone

junction of reason

from a woodcut in the BM

Representation of 'THE WHEEL of FORTUNE'

Taken from a German woodcut c1500

Characters from an Interlude or Dispute: False & True Knowledge c1520

136

# A New Interlude called Jacke Jugeler

Master Boungrace

Dame Coye

Jacke Jugler

Based on a woodcut in the BM

Characters from an Interlude written to be acted by Children. It was first registered at Stationer's Hall in 1562 - because the style of dress indicates a date of c 1500 it was probably being performed before the beginning of the 16th

# Fulgens & Lucrece / Drawn from the Title Page c 1512

138

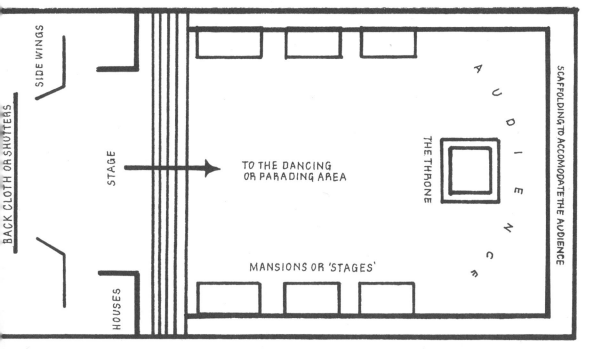

A HALL CONVERTED FOR A COURT MASQUE c1570

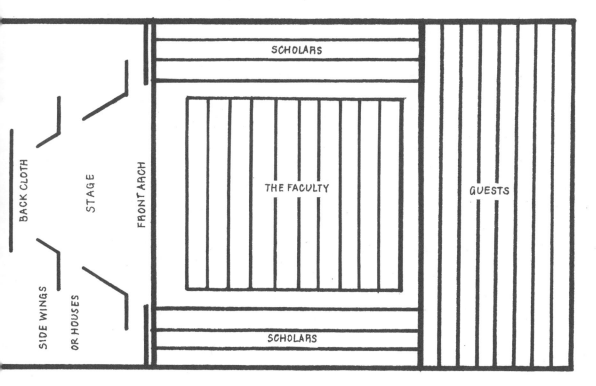

A SCHOOL OR COLLEGE HALL CONVERTED FOR A CLASSICAL PLAY c1570

THE COMEDY SCENE

THE SATIRIC SCENE

THE TRAGEDY SCENE

STAGE SETTINGS
DEVISED BY SERLIO
EMPLOYING THE
ART of PERSPECTIVE

an elaborate and
formal concept rarely
seen in England, except
in a very simplified
manner, until the
performances of
Court masques during
the reign of Charles I

Scenes from a Classical & Historical Play performed in a converted hall c1570 (conjectural)

Conjectural Designs for
Characters from 'Gorboduc' c1570

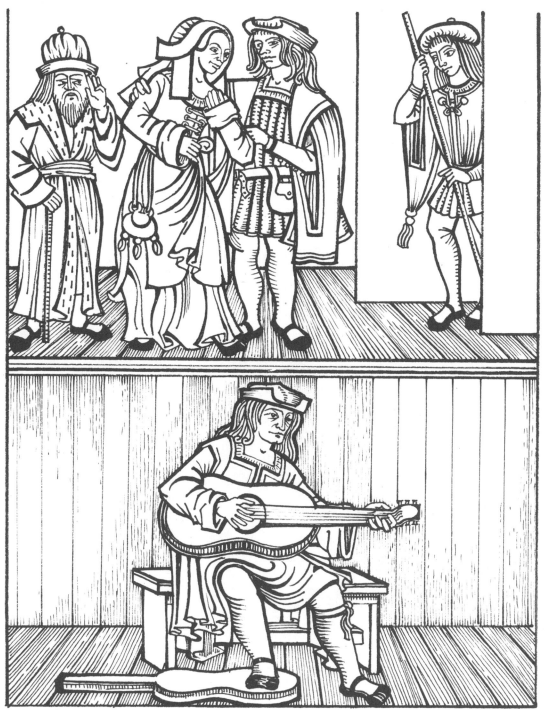

Reconstruction of a Scene from an early C16th Domestic Comedy

143

A Booth Theatre set up by
strolling players in a
Market Square  c1460

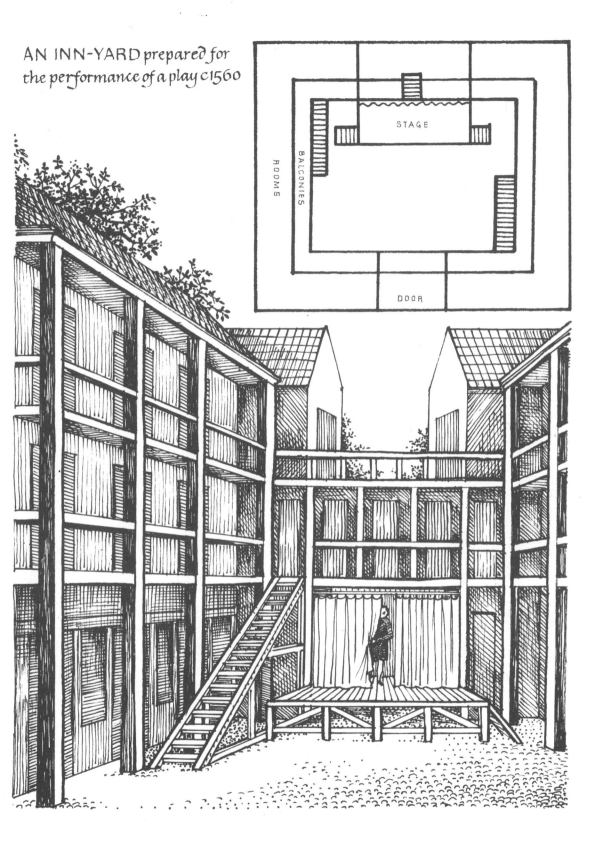

AN INN-YARD prepared for
the performance of a play c1560

STAGE

ROOMS

BALCONIES

DOOR

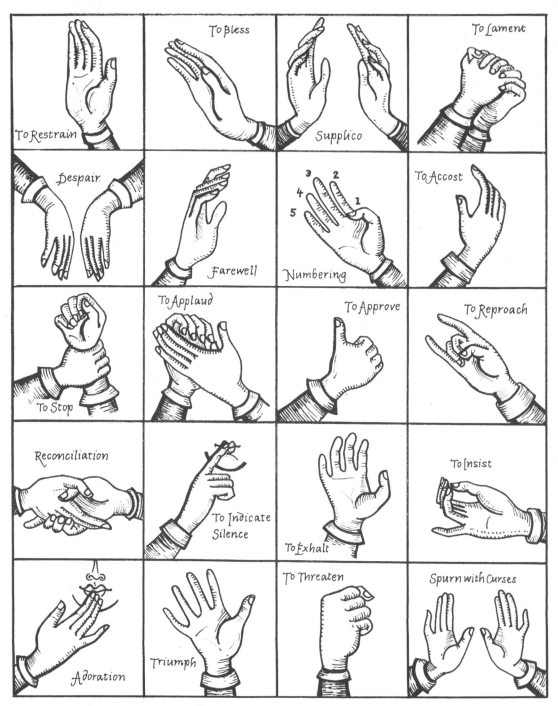

To Restrain — To Bless — Supplico — To Lament

Despair — Farewell — Numbering — To Accost

To Stop — To Applaud — To Approve — To Reproach

Reconciliation — To Indicate Silence — To Exhalt — To Insist

Adoration — Triumph — To Threaten — Spurn with Curses

SOME HAND GESTURES *to support the* Spoken Word *in* ACTING & ORATORY c.1600

146

# 5

# In the Home

## *Courtly Pleasures and Pageantry*

The King, the lords, barons, knights, gentlemen and their ladies rarely watched public entertainments before the 1580s. One of the few occasions when they did watch the common people was at the time of the cycle plays or public executions as described in chapter 3. Even then, they sat apart in comfort in specially built stands decorated with their coats of arms and devices or symbols connected with their families. In later Elizabethan times, young noblemen took to visiting the theatres—but mainly for the bull-baiting sessions or cock-fights. A gentleman might visit a large town fair with his family. In London, the big fair of St Bartholomew in Smith-field was almost matched by that of Southwark. Even in the smaller fairs at Greenwich and the 'May Fair' in what is now London's West End, there were theatrical booths of strolling players (or touring companies). Such a company, or an acrobat, might claim their attention for a few minutes, but actors, musicians and entertainers were normally invited to perform in their castles, halls or houses; large households sometimes employed their own musicians as part of the servant staff, but only the greatest noblemen maintained actors. The Court had its own customs and laws of behaviour, its own dress, its own speech . . . and its own ideas of entertainment.

The duty of the monarch and every knight in medieval England was to protect his people and his country: his whole life was schooled for war and crusades were his delight. When there was no war or crusade to fight, he found his own entertainment in the ancient pleasures of hunting, shooting and fishing, but he also invented for himself and his friends mock battles. These 'tourneys' became theatrical spectacles and festivals as important to the lord of the castle as the cycle plays were to the ordinary people. A flat surface was all he needed for his 'stage', provided at first by a field outside the walls of his castle and later by the courtyard or even at times inside the great hall of his fortified house or palace.

Around the tournament area were stands for the guests (like those built for gentlemen's families to watch the cycle plays), all proudly hung with painted cloths and banners, the symbols related to those sitting in them and to those taking part. All the heraldic colours and metals were used: gold, silver, scarlet, green, blue, black, sanguine (= blood-red) and purple. The performers were the knights and their retainers, resplendent in their armour and coats of arms, which were also worn by the horses carrying them. The tourney was as colourful and rich in emblem and mystic sign and symbol as was the ritual of the Church. Some could be harmless, others could be very rough, with many killed or badly wounded, so dedicated to the contest were those taking part.

In their earliest form the tourneys originated in France during the middle of the eleventh century. Roger of Hevenden, an Englishman, described them as military exercises carried out, 'not in the spirit of hostility, but for practise and display of prowess'. The mock battle involved two large bodies of mounted horsemen who, on the signal from a herald, charged one another from opposite sides, with levelled lances, in what was called the *mêlée*—literally a 'mix-up' in which each individual 'put on show' his skill and courage in combat.

Strict rules controlled the tournament. At the end of the thirteenth century a 'Statute of Arms for Tournaments' decreed that swords with points were not to be used, nor pointed daggers, clubs or maces; a knight who had fallen was to be helped up only by his own squire wearing his device, and anyone who offended was to lose his horse and his arms and be imprisoned. A Court of Honour of royalty and earls was formed to pass judgement on disputants.

The tourney gained great popularity in England despite the condemnation of the Church. Some kings saw the political dangers: Henry II forbade a sport 'which gathered in one place so many barons and knights in arms'; his son, Richard I ('The Lion Heart') granted licences for tournaments to stop his knights from going abroad too often to follow their favourite pastime, and it became a grave offence to arrange a combat without royal licence. To lessen the physical dangers of the sport, sword blades were later made of whalebone and parchment painted silver, and by the fourteenth century lances were either blunted or a protective corona (coronet) was fitted to the end of the weapon. But there were still too many accidents: to the mêlée was added the 'joust', an encounter between two knights, meeting at a slow canter on horse, and attacking each other with blunted sword or lance. If a jouster managed to strike his adversary on either head or breast, or unhorse him, the loser forfeited his horse as a prize to the winner. 'Tilting' was an alternative word for jousting and in this the 'adversary' was later replaced by a suspended ring for the horseman to carry off on the point of his lance, to win a prize given by the ladies who sat behind the 'lists' (palisades enclosing the combat area).

International combats were well known in the fourteenth century. Before the jousts at Windsor on Saint George's Day in 1344, Edward III sent heralds to notify France, Scotland, Burgundy, Hainault, Flanders and Brabant, to allow safe conduct for all competitors. During Edward's reign this commemoration of the Order of the Garter on 23rd April was always accompanied by a tournament in imitation of the Knights of the Round Table. By the sixteenth century, the tournament had developed into a pageant, much like a court masque, and was no longer a serious combat. Knights were always dressing themselves up in fancy dress and we read of one tourney where they appeared disguised as women and as nuns. In 1520, Henry VIII probably staged the most elaborate and greatest tournament of all times when he met Francis I at the Field of Cloth of Gold. Henry was dressed in silver and gold, Francis in gold and brilliant jewels. The festival included every type of knightly tournament. The English king had built a palace some hundred yards square. Around it was the big enclosure for the lists and the grandstands, where the English alone had 2800 tents all of white, topped with their flags, pennants, and standards. A gold statue of Saint Michael stood on a pinnacle. Henry's entourage numbered 4000, and that of his consort, Catherine of Aragon, came to 1200. Cardinal Wolsey, with a retinue of clerics and archers and ushers who carried magnificent gold maces (there were fifty of them), was also attended by one of his household, carrying his great crucifix set with precious stones, dressed in scarlet. Everything was a blaze of colour: cloth of gold and cloth of silver, crimson and scarlet velvets, embroidered and tinselled satins and silks. Heraldry, or the right to 'bear arms,' gave to courtly life a richness of symbol, ornament, colour and decoration, and—for those who could read the symbols—meaning.

Personal devices for identification and recognition go back to the beginning of history. Civil or personal seals, emblems, badges, and insignia, are to be found in all civilisations great or small.

Heraldry has military beginnings in the need to distinguish one party or individual from another. By the twelfth century soldiers were decorating their shields, banners, and pennants with simple and bold devices for easy and, above all else, quick identification in battle, on crusades, and in tournaments. Particularly on crusades, to protect them from the heat of the sun, knights wore surcoats over their metal armour decorated with devices similar to those which covered their shields—hence 'coat of arms'. The horse also wore a coat for protection carrying the same design as that of its rider. A crest, sometimes a different symbol, was attached to the knight's helmet. First made in two dimensions out of metal, it was later modelled in boiled leather mâché or carved in wood in three dimensions, and should the rank of the wearer be superior, he was also permitted to wear his coronet at the base of his crest. Mantling, the foliated material springing from the base of the helmet, is also a reminder of the knight's fighting in the Holy Land, for this, like the surcoat, was a protection from the heat. Twisted into a roll at the base of the crest, the two ends of material (decorated with the colours and emblems of the wearer) opened out to flow down on to the shoulders, covering the back of the head and the neck. So the knight and his horse were covered literally from head to foot in symbolic signs and colours.

Emerging in most European countries by the twelfth century, heraldry had its rules, elements and strict codes which became fixed within the following hundred years. By 1300, England alone had 15,000 distinct coats of arms. Heraldry is indeed a picture-book of instruction and, for those who can read the symbols and order of design, reveals a visual history of the bearer and his family. The elaborate manuals of rules and system of blazoning are complex. Colours, metals and furs are restricted. No colour should be placed on another colour and no metal on a metal—save in the most rare and privileged instances. The most simple devices (probably originating from the mending of shields which had suffered damage on the battle-field with pieces of wood or metal) are called the 'ordinaries'. Patterns, like a chess board or lozenges, filled areas as did stylised representations of various furs (shields early in history may have been covered with furs—the most precious varieties reserved for senior soldiers). Then followed all kinds of natural objects, including plants, beasts, fish and fowl, or only parts of the creatures—and 'strange' creatures like dragons, wyverns, unicorns and griffins.

Blazoning means describing or painting a coat of arms, which consists of:

The Shield—the body
The Helm—the head
The Coronet or Crown—status
The Mantle—the flourish

Supporters—his pages. They usually take the form of beasts and birds
like the lion, tiger, horse, swan, leopard, eagle, ox or deer, etc.

The Motto—the morals by which the owner stands.

Within three or four generations the complexity of adding new devices to
an existing coat of arms required great skill to comply with the firmly
established rules. Badges to distinguish the seniority of sons, or a coat of
arms taken from a conquered province or kingdom or won in battle from an
enemy knight, or belonging to the knight's new wife, or a new 'charge' (any
symbol on the shield) granted for services to king or country, were all in-
corporated into an originally basic and simple scheme.

The wife and children of a knight soon identified themselves with their
husbands or father, and began to cover their robes and mantles with his
symbols and colours, incorporating them with their own.

The Luttrell Psalter (c. 1340) shows Sir Geoffrey Luttrell on his horse
attended by his wife, born Agnes Sutton, wearing her sideless gown decorated with the Luttrell arms impaled with those of Sutton. Accompanying
them is his daughter-in-law, one Beatrice Scrope of Masham. She wears a
similar sideless gown decorated with the arms of Luttrell impaling Scrope
of Masham. Sir Geoffrey's arms decorate not only his shield but also the
banner to his lance, the large square *ailettes* (in modern terminology 'epaul-
ettes'), his surcoat, the fan-crest on his helm, the trapper and fan-crest
worn by his horse, and the saddle. Another example of heraldic splendour
comes from an illuminated picture showing King Henry VIII jousting.
Henry's skirts and horse's mantling are richly embroidered with hearts, the
queen's initial and what looks like affectionate words of love.

Badges worn on the sleeve of servants and retainers symbolised owner-
ship:

> The English are grave like the Germans, lovers of shew: followed wher-
> ever they go by whole troops of servants, who wear their master's arms in
> silver fastened to their left arm.
>
> Paul Hentzner, *Travels in England*, 1598

Lancaster took the red rose for its badge, whilst York took the white, the
two later to be combined in the Tudor Rose. The hog is associated with
Richard III and the white hart with Richard II. The Wiltern Diptych
shows him kneeling in prayer to the Virgin, with the angels surrounding her
dressed in blue and carrying on their sleeves an image of Richard's white
hart. He loved badges. A painting of him in Westminster Abbey shows him

crowned, wearing a blue gown embroidered all over with his initial 'R' surmounted by a crown, alternating with a foliated rosette; he also used a sunburst and a sprig of genista for identification. All, including humble workers, could be identified by what they wore, the type of material and its cut, and the colours and the amount of cloth or fur permitted by laws, or habits, formed during the thirteenth and fourteenth centuries. Some laws determined the length of a train, the quantity and type of fur, the correct cut of the beard, and the length of the points of the shoes. Brooches, a cockle-shell, chains about the shoulders, a glove pinned to a hat, or a scarf tied about the upper part of a gentleman's arm all conveyed a message.

At the time of the Tudors the 'field' (background of the shield, surcoat, sideless gown, banner, etc.) was literally filled with a complex of sometimes up to a dozen different bearings collected by the family during the previous three centuries. Heraldry by 1500 was, though rarely seen in battle, used everywhere: decorating the house, the chapel, furniture, enamel-work, engraved on glass, carved on stone or wood, woven into embroideries and tapestries, worked into plaster decorations, and silver and gold were embossed with it. Universities and schools, cities and boroughs, guilds, bishops and priests—all wanted their own coats of arms. Heralds, pages and livery-men bore the colours and/or the badge of whom they served, declaring their allegiance.

The duties of a herald, displaying the coat of arms of his master on his tabard, grew from 'heraldry' (that is, calling out the name of his knight) at a tournament to involvement in almost all aspects of court and knightly life. The king employed many and, by the sixteenth century, the heralds had almost as much control as the ecclesiastical courts over ceremony, behaviour and protocol on great occasions. To this day, the Duke of Norfolk (with his Arundel Herald) stage-manages all major state and royal ceremonies—weddings, funerals and coronations—and the armed forces still stage an annual 'Royal Tournament'. The tournament was the most lavish of all royal and noble entertainments.

Inside his castle, palace or house, the lord and his lady entertained themselves and their guests, particularly during and after eating and drinking. The castle's basic function was to provide safety. Comfort was sacrificed for security. It housed the lord and his family, their household and servants. It was also a barracks for the men at arms. It housed the armourers, the horse, and the makers and repairers of machinery and devices of war. Architecturally the whole design was conceived to protect and make it an object as difficult as possible to penetrate by enemy and invader. By the end of the Wars of the Roses the nobility began to build themselves large houses for a self-contained community life—they were built for peace and not for war. There were now gardens of flowers and herbs, with orchards, vegetable gardens, arbours and loggias, dove-cots and beehives, ornamental pools, and little fountains, all neat and geometric in design. In bad weather the family exercised and played simple games and gossiped in the long gallery of the house, but when the sun shone there were the covered walks and the little walled courtyards in which to spend the mornings and afternoons. Here one could sew and embroider, sing and make music, and entertain. Sweet-smelling wild and cultivated plants and flowers like the violet and pansy, the little iris, and the clove-scented pink, or the wild strawberry, grew in profusion along the top of, and in and amongst, the little walls. Red, white and pink musk-roses trailed their way about the trellised arbours.

It is typical of the English that all, rich or poor, enjoy their gardens, orchards, and the countryside. William Harrison writes in 1587:

> If you look into our gardens annexed to our houses, how wonderfully is their beauty increased, not only with flowers . . . and variety of curious and costly workmanship, but also with rare and medicinable herbs sought up in the land within these forty years. How art also helpeth nature in the daily colouring, doubling and enlarging the proportion of our flowers, it is incredible to report . . . herbs fetched out of other regions near hand, insomuch that I have seen in some one garden to the number of three or four hundred of them . . . And even as it fareth with our gardens, so doth it with our orchards . . . most delicate apples, plums, pears, walnuts, filberts. etc., strange fruit, as apricots, almonds, peaches, figs, corn-trees in noblemen's orchards. I have seen capers, oranges and lemons, and heard of wild olives growing here beside other strange trees brought from afar, whose names I know not.

It is not hard to understand why flowers, and their 'meaning', became so important to the Elizabethans, who loved wearing them and used them so regularly as signs and symbols in their decorative arts, including, in particular, their embroideries and jewellery.

As in the design of a castle, the great hall of the house was the most important room other than the chapel. This hall was always rectangular, hung with painted cloths or tapestries, depending on the wealth of the owner, which depicted scenes from the Bible, the four seasons of the year, or esoteric and allegorical themes and stories from the civilisations of Rome and Greece. Decorative patterns were also stencilled or freely drawn on to the painted cloths, diapered with heraldic and symbolic motifs associated with the family: beasts, flowers, badges or flowing foliated patterns in the heraldic colours. The overhead beams and wooden roof were similarly carved and painted, one very popular theme being the signs of the Zodiac. Rushes, sweet-smelling fronds of lavender, herbs and wild flowers were scattered over the flagged floor. Permanent furniture was minimal—a dias at one end, a chair, a few stools—but at noon and in the evening the hall was prepared for dinner with flares and with hoops of candles suspended from the roof to give light.

At the west end occupied by the dais, a long trestle-table, running almost the full width of the building, was set up, covered by a fine tablecloth. Here sat the master of the house, occupying the only chair (from which custom is derived our surviving use of the word 'chairman'); his family and his guests of honour sat on stools or benches. This high table displayed his finest possessions: goblets, ewers, and plate, sometimes of gold. The most magnificent ornaments were the containers for spices and the great salt-cellars. Guests supplied their own knives but were provided with a spoon. Only the very richest and most fashionable had a fork. They frequently shared the same cup, a ceremony sometimes remembered at banquets in the City of London today in passing round 'the loving cup', and they normally ate off wooden trenchers. White cloths and ewers of water were provided for washing hands. Members of the household and less important guests sat at shorter trestle tables running at right angles to the high table. Seated according to rank, they were supplied with food only after high table had been served. On the arrival of the food from the kitchens (the bearers sometimes having walked long distances along open paths) minstrels blew trumpets, and a blessing was asked, followed by silence. All important dishes were presented first to the high table, always accompanied by a reverence—the bending of the knees.

Food was treated with great respect. It had taken a vast number of the household to prepare and it was precious. Wines were mixed with honey or ginger; all sorts of animal flesh, fowl and game (including thrushes, gulls, herons, vultures, peacocks and swans) were eaten as well as fish, a few vegetables, wild and cultivated fruits, and pastries. Bread, served wrapped in white cloths, was originally also the poor man's plate. (Many people in southern Europe and Scandinavia still eat quite large meals on pieces of open bread in the medieval manner without realising it.) It was hard to keep food fresh, but some form of preservation was adopted by burying meat, fish and fowl in a cloth in the earth. (In England today game is still occasionally buried in its own grave until ready.) Salt and precious spices from the East, however, were the common preservatives. Most of the food was chopped up finely, coloured, and heavily spiced, then moulded into fanciful shapes to make it look more palatable in spite of the long time it may have been kept. A lot of alcohol was consumed during the course of the meal and any noble-man worth his salt (that is, able to own a beautiful salt-cellar) would also provide music for his guests. If he were rich enough he would have built a gallery at the end of the hall facing the high table, to house the minstrels or bands of players. They played on a small selection of soft-sounding instru-ments to contrast with the trumpeters who 'heralded' each course: reed pipes, recorders, tabor, fiddles or viols, bells or bagpipes. Lutes, from the Middle East crusades, came later, and there may also have been a small harp and a portative organ. After the meal, when food had filled the belly and drink had mellowed the mind, came the time for the less intellectual enter-tainment. Inhibitions and protocol were dismissed, the lower tables (and their occupants) were removed and the evening's entertainment really started. Games like blind-man's-buff, leap-frog, 'ring-a-ring-a-roses', parading and blowing out lighted tapers, catching a ball, and 'squeak piggy squeak' were played somewhat more lustily than our present children's party versions.

On certain feast days, a 'Lord of Misrule' was elected to encourage the guests to misbehave (as some clerics did during 'The Feast of the Boy Bishop' or 'The Feast of the Fools'). During the long Christmas cel-ebrations (from mid-December to the beginning of January) 'the Lord' was the master of ceremonies who organised the games and amusements. In his after-supper games, the English medieval courtier was hard to recognise as the chivalrous knight of Norman ancestry brought up on rules of courtly love and the worship of the Virgin. Courtly love may have been brought back by the crusaders, influenced by Arabic philosophy, which was mystical in content and concept. There is little doubt that Arabic ideas and literature spread from Muslim Spain into the south of France and up into the Northern Courts of Europe, where the troubadours evolved their romantic esoteric court songs and poetry.

The troubadours, singing their ballads of courtly love and chivalry, seem not to have greatly impressed English lords. But the hangers-on of the troubadour's retinue—the acrobats, tumblers, mimes and dancers—appear in English noble houses as 'mummers', allying their talents to the age-old pagan rituals. Favourite characters included Saint George (good), his enemy (evil), Robin Hood (the countryman's friend), Maid Marian (fertility), a comic doctor (resurrection) and various animal disguises. Mummer's plays were passed on by word of mouth—texts appear only late in the eighteenth century. Records of these performances occur over the whole of the British Isles—and the reason for lack of early texts is perhaps that most of the plays had no words and relied solely on mime, dance and popular songs.

Fools and jesters were licensed and in the retinue of kings, clerics, and wealthy lords. They also encouraged misbehaving against normal authority; some were hunch-backed, and some were dwarfs dressed in fancy clothes to amuse the ladies. Some say they were inspired madmen. In England their origin seems to come from the clown or 'Vice', the character from the old religious plays who made fun of the Devil and played tricks on the more serious characters. Feste, the professional fool to Olivia in *Twelfth Night*, sings:

'Like to the old Vice,
Your need to sustain;
Who, with dagger of lath,
In his rage and his wrath,
Cries, ah, ha! to the devil.'

The nobility also entertained themselves, dressing up and playing at amateur theatricals: they sang, they acted and they danced. The wearing of fancy-dress and disguising with a mask goes far back into history and is connected with early rituals and folk plays. The mummers, particularly those following Italian customs, were often disguised visitors or guests with blackened faces or wearing masks and visors, and would arrive bearing presents for their host who, with the members of *his* household, danced with them in return. The Italian masque with its elaborate staging, ornamental speech, song, music and dancing, and magnificent costumes and scenery, was introduced by Henry VIII to his Court, replacing the more mystical rustic masking and mumming.

The Court rarely danced in the early Middle Ages. Dancing was considered the peasants' pastime, or it may have been a question of lack of space in the great hall, for it was not until the fourteenth century that the central stone hearth, with a hole in the ceiling above to let out the smoke, was moved to the side of the hall, becoming a fire-place, to give greater space for the pleasure of dancing. Before this (and they must have been a hardy people to withstand the cold, wrapping themselves up in their heavy fur-lined robes and mantles) dancing would have been partially improvised, moving in one or more circles around the hearth. This kind of round dance is common to all civilisations.

With the removal of the central hearth, the dance began to become experimental in figures, steps and groupings. But it was not very skilful, and as long as you got to your right place at the right time it did not matter very much how you managed it . . . provided you were ready with your reverence. Many were processional, the dancers in pairs moving slowly up to the high table and then back again down the full length of the hall. The earliest of the dances was the *ductia*, accompanied probably on loud instruments, and then came the *estampie*, accompanied on strings or keyboard—before this time dances were often unaccompanied save for the songs sung by the performers themselves.

By the fifteenth century the great court employed their own composers who were ready to prepare music for all the important occasions, and sometimes works were commissioned by musicians from foreign countries. Small bands accompanied the dance, playing what we would now call oboes and trombones. This century brings with it the *basse-dance* (a blanket-term for all dances accompanied on 'soft' instruments), with organised rules. Steps were now grouped together in measures, forming patterns of twos and threes. Two new dances monopolised the sixteenth century. The first—supposedly from Padua was a proud processional dance for the young and the old to display their elegance. Called the pavan in England, it was performed in slow quadruple time, at weddings, funerals, ceremonies at law courts and universities, any gentleman's party, and all Court functions. The second dance was quicker, more spirited and performed in triple time—the galliard.

These were the last of the 'elitist' dances, for, despite shocking imports such as the volta (in which man and woman faced each other in each other's arms for the first time in a Court dance), the Elizabethan Court preferred to follow Her Majesty in the processional dance and imitate the country dances of the peasants in their private houses. She loved 'show' and 'display' not only whilst at Court but also on her many progresses to her various palaces and the houses of her nobles—just as Becket in the twelfth century had enjoyed going to France to arrange the marriage of Henry II's son. He took with him some two hundred of his own household—knights, squires, clergy, servants, pages and soldiers all magnificently dressed—

with dogs walking beside the horses, who wore silver bits in their mouths. Eight carriages drawn by horse carried presents to the French King. Horses also were carriers of silver plate, books and altar furnishings. Monkeys accompanied them dressed in rich livery! On their arrival in France it is said that over two hundred singing boys marched six abreast to accompany them.

'The Great Gloriana' similarly, on her progresses, was accompanied by her great Court, her retainers, heralds, and her officers, all wearing their ceremonial dress. At intervals on these journeys plays, entertainments, and pageants were given for her enjoyment—with singing, music, dancing and fine visual display. These huge and costly progresses were slowly replacing, for the people in the provinces and the countryside, their own performances of the cycle plays which were being 'phased out' by civic and church authority.

By the 1590s, the young gentlemen were again thinking only of war, and their tastes in entertainment seldom went beyond gambling or the dog-fights and bull- and bear-baiting. Paul Hentzner, writing in 1598, states:

There is still another place, built in the form of a theatre, which serves for the baiting of bears [sometimes the teeth of the bear were broken prior to performance] and bulls. They are fastened behind, and, then worried by those great English dogs and mastiffs, but not without great risk to the dogs from the teeth of the one and the horns of the other: and it sometimes happens they are killed on the spot. Fresh ones are immediately supplied in the place of those wounded or tired. To this entertainment there often follows that of whipping a blinded bear, which is performed by five or six men, standing in a circle with whips, which they exercise upon him without mercy. Although he cannot escape from them because of his chain, he nevertheless defends himself, vigorously throwing down all who come within his reach and are not active enough to get out of it, and tearing the whips out of their hands and breaking them.

It is paradoxical that the so-called 'Golden Age' of English music and drama should have had such a cruel background of popular entertainment and that so many lords—and ladies—preferred the crude game to the cultured pastime.

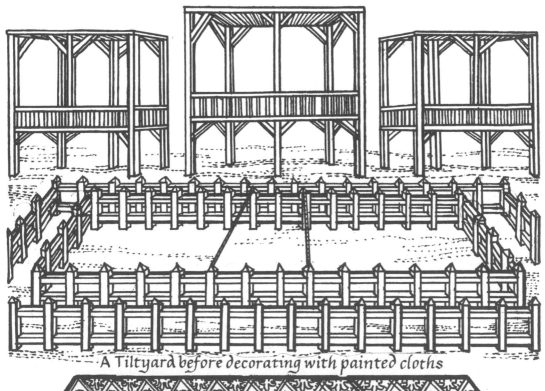
A Tiltyard before decorating with painted cloths

TILTING IN PROGRESS c 1520

159

KNIGHTS
PREPARING
FOR THE MÉLÉE

15th

A KNIGHT PREPARED
FOR THE TOURNAMENT

Music accompanying the investiture of a Knight

Taken from an illuminated manuscript drawing C13th

## Ceremonial Dress at Court incorporating Heraldry

(left) the coat of arms of Margaret of Anjou impaled with the arms of her husband Henry VI.
(above) the coat of arms of Ann Neville impaled with the arms of her husband, Richard III.

THE **ARMS OF**
THE CITY OF CANTERBURY

THE **ARMS OF**
BALLIOL COLLEGE OXFORD

THE ARMS **OF THE**
WORSHIPFUL **COMPANY**
OF HABERDASHERS LONDON
1503

THE **ARMS OF**
THE PROVINCE OF CANTERBURY

Griffin   Dragon
*4 mythological beasts*

THE **ARMS**
OF ETON

*cockatrice*

*wyvern*

The Banner of TALBOT, Earl of SHREWSBURY

164

PER FESS

FESS

BARS

PER BEND

PER PALE

PALE

PALLETS

BEND

QUARTERLY    PER SALTIRE    PER CHEVRON

CROSS    SALTIRE    CHEVRON

the armourial bearings of John Beaufort, Duke of Somerset

SOME HERALDIC ORDINARIES

165

HENRY BOLINGBROKE'S STANDARD

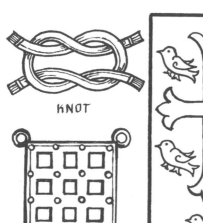

KNOT

PORTCULLIS

The Royal Arms impaled with those of Edward the Confessor

WATER BOUGET

WHEATSHEAF

PLANTA GENISTA

SUNBURST

Badges associated with Richard II - the White Hart

# BADGES, BANNERS and STANDARDS

ROYAL PAGEANTRY THROUGH THE STREETS c1480

ROYAL PAGEANTRY ON THE RIVER THAMES c1480

# ROYAL PAGEANTRY

Henry VIII on his way to the

The English Rose

The Red Rose of Lancaster

The White Rose of York

based on a painting in the BM

...g of Parliament

The Red and White Tudor Rose

Elizabethan Coronet of Roses

169

QUEEN ELIZABETH I on PROGRESS

from a drawing in the BM

PAGEANT WAGON carrying VENUS c1575

SPORTS & PASTIME: Bear & Stag Baiting (stag baiting was very popular in Rome)

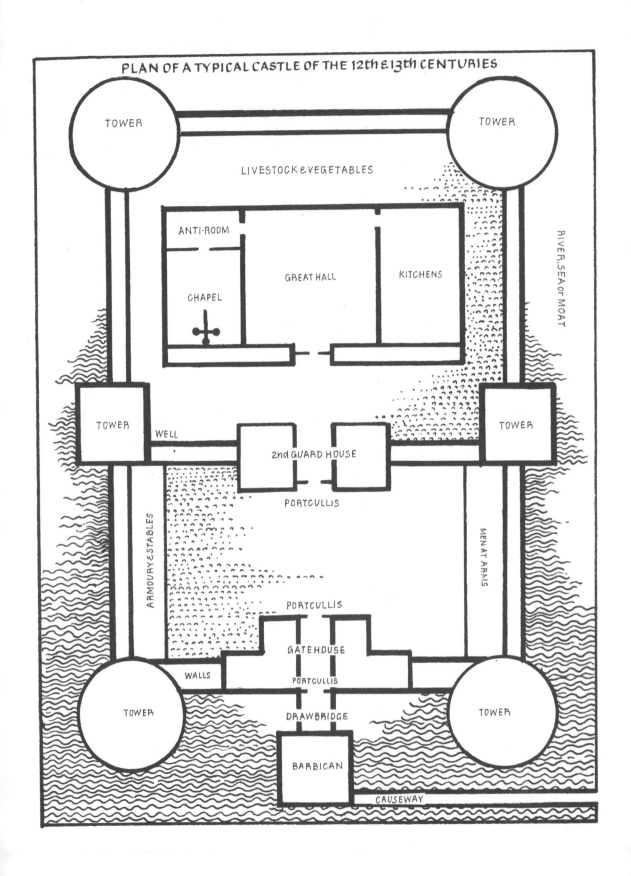

PLAN OF A TYPICAL CASTLE OF THE 12th & 13th CENTURIES

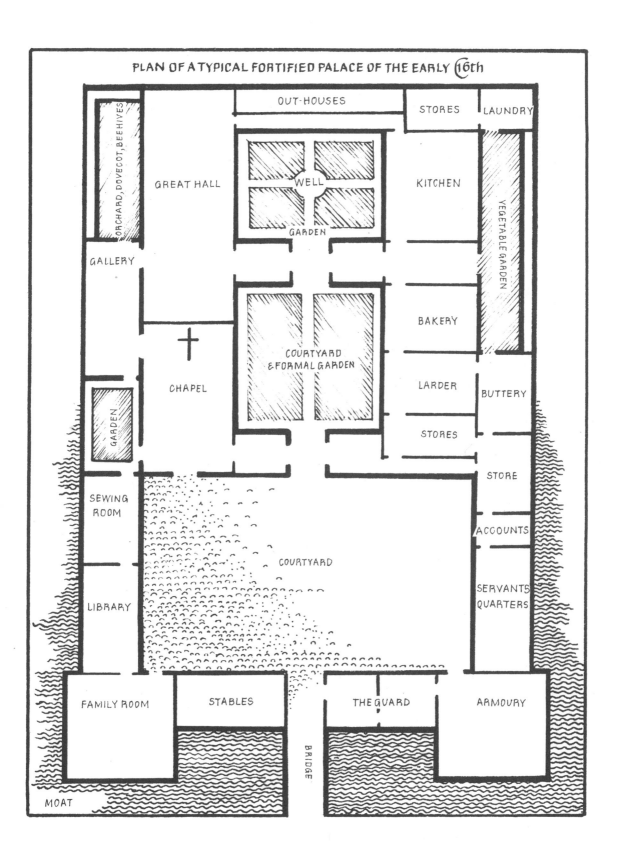

PLAN OF A TYPICAL FORTIFIED PALACE OF THE EARLY 16th

OUT-HOUSES

STORES

LAUNDRY

ORCHARD, DOVECOT, BEEHIVES

GREAT HALL

WELL

GARDEN

KITCHEN

VEGETABLE GARDEN

GALLERY

CHAPEL

COURTYARD & FORMAL GARDEN

BAKERY

LARDER

BUTTERY

STORES

GARDEN

STORE

SEWING ROOM

COURTYARD

ACCOUNTS

LIBRARY

SERVANTS QUARTERS

FAMILY ROOM

STABLES

THE GUARD

ARMOURY

BRIDGE

MOAT

The Great Hall, Hampton Court Palace

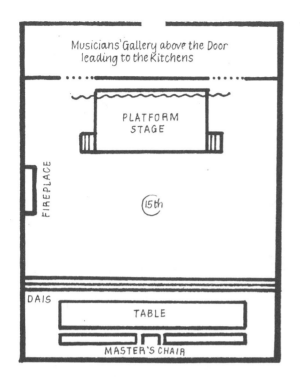

Musicians'Gallery above the Door
leading to the Kitchens

PLATFORM STAGE

FIREPLACE

15th

DAIS

TABLE

MASTER'S CHAIR

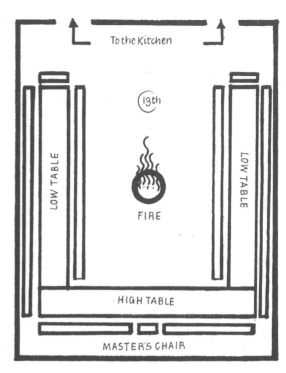

To the Kitchen

13th

LOW TABLE

FIRE

LOW TABLE

HIGH TABLE

MASTER'S CHAIR

## RECONSTRUCTED PLANS OF A GREAT HALL prepared for eating & entertainments

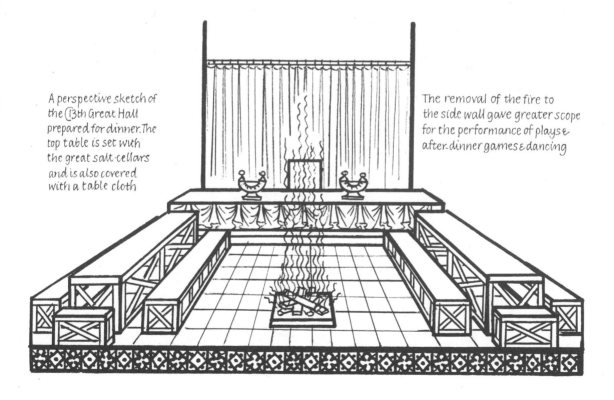

A perspective sketch of the 13th Great Hall prepared for dinner. The top table is set with the great salt-cellars and is also covered with a table cloth

The removal of the fire to the side wall gave greater scope for the performance of plays & after-dinner games & dancing

A Mediaeval Banquet C14th

THE COURT DANCING C15th

14th Musical Instruments

Psaltery

Hurdy Gurdy

Mandolin

Reed Pipe

Bones

Kettle Drums

Bagpipes

Viol

Portative Organ

Drum

Viol

C14th Musical Instruments

Trumpets

Double Pipes

Tambourine

Jesters

13th

14th

15th

16th

from early manuscripts

RECONSTRUCTION of a COURT MASQUE as seen from the stage

Based on a woodcut in the BM

C16th Moated House & Garden

Everything in a Garden to entertain the Five Senses c1500

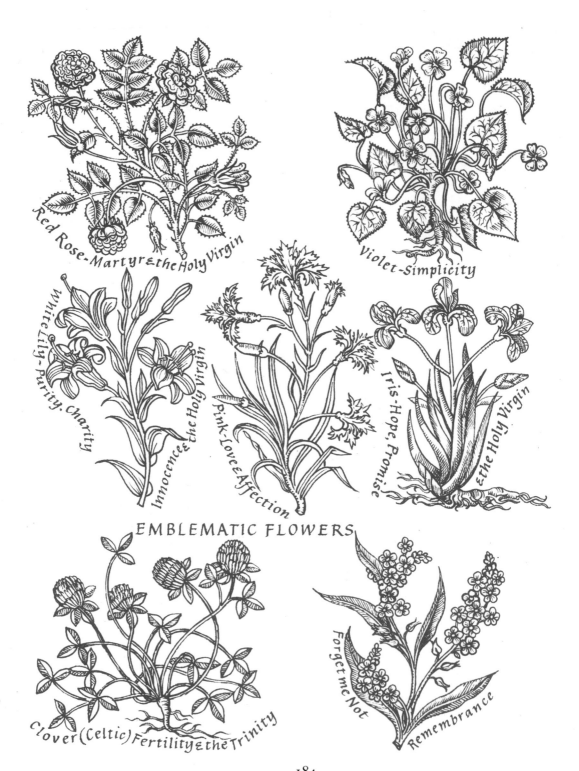

Red Rose-Martyr & the Holy Virgin

Violet-Simplicity

White Lily-Purity. Charity

Innocence & the Holy Virgin

Pink-Love & Affection

Iris-Hope, Promise & the Holy Virgin

EMBLEMATIC FLOWERS

Clover (Celtic) Fertility & the Trinity

Forget me Not

Remembrance

# 6

# 𝕴𝖓 𝖙𝖍𝖊 𝕮𝖔𝖚𝖓𝖙𝖗𝖞𝖘𝖎𝖉𝖊

*Underground Theatre, Secret Worship, and Dancing*

Against May, Whitsunday, or some other time of the year, every parish, town and village assemble themselves together, both men, women and children, old and young, even all indifferently; and either going all together or dividing themselves into companies, they go some to the woods and groves, some to the hills and mountains, some to one place and some to another, where they spend all the night in pleasant passtimes; and in the morning they return, bringing with them birch boughs and branches of trees, to deck their assemblies withal. And no marvel, for there is a great lord present among them, as superintendent and lord over their passtimes and sports, namely *Sathan*, prince of Hell. But their chiefest jewel they bring from thence is their May-Pole, which they bring home with great veneration, as thus. They have twenty or fourty yoke of oxen, every ox having a sweet nosegay of flowers placed on the tip of his horns; and these oxen draw home this may-pole (this stinking idol rather) which is covered all over with flowers and herbs, bound round about with strings from the top to the bottom, and sometimes painted with variable colours, with two or three hundred men, women and children following it with great devotion. And thus being reared up with handkerchiefs and flags streaming on the top, they straw the ground about, bind green boughs about it, set up summer-halls, bowers and arbours hard by it; and then they fall to banquet and feast, to leap and dance about it, as the heathen people did at the dedication of their idols, whereof this is a perfect pattern, or rather the thing itself . . .

. . . I have heard it credibly reported (and that viva voce) by men of great gravitie and reputation, that of fortie, three-score, or a hundred maids going to the woods over night, there have scarcely the third part of them return home again undefiled!

[Stubbes, *Anatomy of Abuses*, 1583 (Second Edition)]

185

Even allowing for Stubbes's Puritanical zeal, there is no doubt that country festivals in England throughout the Middle Ages were observances of pagan antiquity and were basically fertility rites. The most important were the May rites, originally centred on a bush, a mound or a tree, but by the later Middle Ages around a specially prepared 'maypole'. A tree-trunk was stripped of its leaves and branches, then redecorated with flowers and, fastened to the top, long ribbons. The dancers, holding these streamers, wound their way in and out around its base in a circle, eventually weaving a sheath of intricately manipulated patterns of ribbon to cover the trunk completely. The central character in these rites was either Robin of the Hood or Jack in the Green (the spirit of the woods) who, covered with leaves and flowers, danced through the village to the sound of voices and musical instruments. At the end of the ceremonies he was symbolically drowned—a fertility power of life-forces given by his death to the people of the village.

May-rites occurred after seed-time in Anglo-Saxon England and they were also, in pagan times, consecrated to Hertha, goddess of peace and fertility. Each village, in the absence of the master, enjoyed electing a 'Lord' or 'King', who in turn chose his 'Queen'. He wore an oak and she a haw-thorn wreath. Together they gave laws to the rustic sports during their days of Freedom. Young men regularly, as a sign or talisman, gathered branches and fastened them to their sweethearts' doors; wells were dressed with the fronds of leaves and with flowers, accompanied with a blessing.

A survival of one of England's processional dances which led the village to the Maypole was 'Green-Garters'; known to have been danced in the churchyards during the late twelfth century, it continued in Wales until well into the last century.

The Church's connection with many of these ceremonies was uneasy. Although they were officially condemned, these were the people's rites and parish priests knew that their hold was too strong to break. Besides, the lords of the manor were often in sympathy with their own peasants, and, as Stubbes continued his testimony:

All the wild heads of the parish, conventing together, choose them a Grand Captain whom they enoble with the title of My Lord of Misrule, and him they crown with great solemnity, and adopt for their king. This king anointed, chooseth forth twenty, forty, three-score or a hundred lusty guts, like himself, to wait upon his lordly majesty, and to guard his noble person. Then, every one of these his men, he investeth with his liveries of green, yellow, or some other light wanton colour; as though they were not bawdy-gawdy enough I should say, they bedeck themselves with scarfs, ribbons and laces hanged all over with gold rings, precious stones and other jewels; this done, they ties about either leg twenty or fourty bells, with rich handkerchiefs in their hands, and sometimes laid across their shoulders and necks, borrowed for the most part of their pretty Mopsies and loving Bessies, for bussing them in the dark. Thus all things set in order, they have they their hobby-horses, dragons and other antics, together with their bawdy pipers and thundering drummers to strike up the *devil's* dance withal. Then march these heathen company towards the church and church-yard, their pipers piping, their drummers thundering, their stumps dancing, their bells jingling, their handkerchiefs swinging about their heads like madmen, their hobby-horses and other monsters skirmishing amongst the throng; and in this sort they go to the church (I say) and into the church (though the minister be at prayer or preaching) dancing and swinging their handkerchiefs, over their heads in the church, like devils incarnate, with such a confused noise, that no man can hear his own voice . . . . Then, after this, about the church they go again and again, and so forth into the church yard, where they have commonly their summer-hals, their bowers, arbours, and banqueting houses set up, wherein they feast, banquet and dance all that day and (peradventure) all the night too. And thus these terrestrial furies spend the Sabbath day.

They have also certain papers, wherein is painted some babblery or other of imagery work, and these they call 'My Lord of Misrule's badges'; these they give to everyone that will give money for them to maintain them in their heathenry, devilry, whoredom, drunkeness, pride, and what not.

The hobby-horse was a survival of earlier animal worship and was ridden by one of the dancers, whilst the 'fool' wore a tail. Another surviving aspect of its origins as a fertility right was the belief that any woman who touched the horse or was caught under its skirts would be favoured in childbearing. The bells worn by the dancers were meant to frighten evil spirits. Although the dancing became known as 'morris dancing'—supposedly brought to England by Edward III from 'Moorish' Spain—animal dances of this kind are known from ancient Egyptian and Greek civilisations at least. A very early example of the horn dance survives still in the annual re-creation of the Abbots Bromley Dance in Staffordshire. This dance is part hunting dance, part fertility rite, and part contest between good and evil. A twenty mile circuit, out to the local farms, is covered by the group, which consists of six men each carrying a reindeer skull complete with antlers, a fool, a hobby-horse, and a man dressed up to represent Maid Marian.

The 'horned god' cult in England, according to information coming chiefly from ecclesiastical and judicial documents, associated the 'god' with the Devil or Satan. Worship is recorded in 1303 when the Bishop of Coventry was accused of doing homage to the Devil dressed to look like a sheep. Herne the Hunter with his head-springing antlers, the phantom rider accompanied by his pack of phantom dogs, was seen regularly in the great woods of Windsor. The Devil always appeared in public in his own clothes and only 'transformed' himself when in the presence of his initiates to resemble a bull or stag, sometimes a ram or goat, dog or horse; he always presented himself in animal form. The Puck Fair, held at Killorglin in Ireland, was presided over by a male goat attended by young boys dressed in green and the ram, a symbol of strength and energy, was regularly presented as a prize to those who won in wrestling combats. Chaucer writes: 'At wrastlynge he wolde bere awey the ram'.

Robin Hood, Goodfellow, or Puck as he was variously known, was represented as half-man, half-beast with horns until well into the seventeenth century. His attendants were dressed in green, the colour of the fairies, which could also symbolise both fertility and bad luck. His power was too much for Bishop Latimer in the 1540s:

I came once myself to a place, riding on a journey home-ward from London, and I sent word over night into the town that I would preach there in the morning because it was holy day, and methought it was an holy day's work. The church stood in my way, and I took my horse, and my company, and went thither. I thought I should have found a great company in the church, and when I came there, the church door was fast locked.

I tarried there half an hour or more, at last the key was found, and one of the parish comes to me and says 'Sir, this is a busy day with us, we cannot hear you, it is Robin Hood's day. The parish are gone abroad to gather for Robin Hood. I pray you let them not'. I thought my rochet should have been regarded, though I were not, but it would not serve, it was fain to give place to Robin Hood's men. It is no laughing matter my friends, it is a weeping matter, a heavy matter, under the pretence for gathering for Robin Hood, a traitor, and a thief, to put out a preacher, to have his office less esteemed, to prefer Robin Hood before the ministration of God's word, and all this hath come of unpreaching prelates.

Robin Hood and Jack of the Green appeared as characters in mummers' plays (see chapter 5) and village actors performed many playlets or simple scenes linked with other festivals, especially those of Christmas—a ransom to the Church—and, in farming communities, on Plough Monday (when the lord of the manor gave a final feast after Christmas before ploughing began again). The Lord Mayor of London still keeps up the tradition of Plough Monday Dinner, when he entertains 'servants' of the Corporation of London. The plays were passed on by one generation to the next, usually by word of mouth. 'Saint George and the Dragon' was a favourite, accompanied by round dances with drums and fifes (representing the eternal struggle of good over evil). The performance of *Pyramus and Thisbe* by Quince and his rustic companions before Theseus in *A Midsummer Night's Dream* is a classic example of this type of playlet: a prologue where all the characters are introduced, the play itself, the return of all the characters (Resurrection) followed by a dance, and lastly the hope of remuneration for their work. Often included in these entertainments was a sword dance, which some claim is tied up with early morris or Moorish dances. The Revesby and Shetland Sword dances, recorded as late as the eighteenth century, were acted out by plough-boys and morris dancers with their costumes garnished with ribbons. They all carried swords and followed a leader or master, progressing in intricate patterns until all the swords were locked together so that they could all be held up by the hilt of a single sword.

The 'magic' contained in these dances was something that even the dancer could not explain or understand. Because there was something outside the world around him which only dancing seemed to contact—like private prayer—so dancing was pursued in secret.

PSALM 149: Praise ye the Lord, Sing unto the Lord a new song and his praise in the congregation of Saints . . . . Let them praise his name in the *dance*: let them sing praises unto him with the timbrel and harp. For the Lord taketh *pleasure* in his people.

PSALM 150: Praise him the sound of the trumpet; praise him with the psaltery and harp. Praise him with the timbrel and *dances*: praise him with stringed instruments and organs. Praise him upon the loud cymbals: praise him upon the high sounding cymbals. Let everything that hath breath praise the Lord. Praise *ye* the Lord. [Author's italics]

There were three basic patterns for the dance: the round or circle dance; the processional dance; and the labyrinth or spiral dance. But they all had a leader to follow. England's processional Furry dance takes place with the performers holding hands to form a chain, winding their way in and out of every room and every house in the village, copying and following their leader.

Circular dances are known to have been performed in churches around the altar—probably relics of the old Roman festival of Lupercalia and the round dance of the stars. Dancing was the creation of the gods 'and should at all times be honoured'. The old ball game in the church was supposed to follow the path or 'dance' of the sun. Some say that it originated in an early custom based on fertility rites; others, that the ball was originally the severed head of an enemy to be kicked around as an act of joy. (Severed heads were set up by the Celts to defend their sacred places.) The game, or sacred ritual, took place at Easter. The Reverend George S. Tyack's *Lore and Legend of the English Church*, published in 1895, states:

Among other places it is recorded to have taken place at Chester Cathedral on Easter Monday . . . . It was conducted in a fashion which implies that it had some religious significance, and was in fact considered at its commencement as a religious ceremony. The deacon received the ball, and immediately began to chant an antiphon, moving meanwhile in a stately step in time to the music; then with his left hand he tossed, or handed the ball to another of the clergy; when it had reached the hands of the dean, he threw it in turn to the choristers, the antiphon, accompanied by the organ, meanwhile continuing. The statutes of the cathedrals regulated the size of the balls used in this strange rite.

As we have already seen, Church authorities were constantly trying to get dancing out of the church and to suppress the dance, until it finally moved into the streets, then to the countryside and to secret places by the early Middle Ages. Bishop Richard Poore of Salisbury in the thirteenth century prohibited all dancing or vile indecorous games which 'tempt to unseemliness'.

HE gathered all of us together and said:
Before I am delivered up unto them,
Let us sing a hymn to the Father,
And go forth to that which lieth before us.

190

He bade us therefore make as it were a ring,
holding one another's hands,
And himself standing in the midst he said:
Answer Amen unto me.
He began then to sing an hymn and to say:
Glory be to thee, Father.
And we, *going about in a ring*, answered him: Amen
    . . . Graces danceth. I would pipe; *dance* ye all. Amen.
I would mourn. Lament ye all. Amen
The number Eight singeth praise with us. Amen.
The number Twelve *danceth* on high. Amen.
The whole on high hath part in *our dancing*. Amen.
Who so *danceth* not, knoweth not what cometh to pass. Amen.

[Author's italics]

The above is part of the mystical dance of Jesus described in the Apocry-
phal Acts of Saint John. During the fourth century Augustine makes
reference to this dance which, during his life, was still held sacred as a
ritual of initiation. 'Christ', or the leader and all-knowing one, stands in the
centre whilst his disciples walk, sing and dance in a circle around him,
copying all of his actions. Such danced hymns were banned by the Church
but were still performed in Christian communities away from the official
body. It was celebrated after the Sacred Meal when Christ asks his disciples
to follow him in exactly everything that he does: 'Now answer thou (or as
thou respondest unto my dancing). Behold thyself in me who speak and
seeing what I do . . . keep silent about my mysteries.'

Many of the clandestine dances were associated with 'fairies', a term far
more real to man in the Middle Ages than that reserved for children today.
The labyrinth or spiral dance was walked (or stepped) to imitate a wandering spirit, identified in early Christian times with Satan. From the eleventh
century on, labyrinths were inlaid in the floor of many a European church's
nave, so that Satan's path could be taken and resisted. Medieval England
had hundreds of mazes up and down the country, usually cut into the turf,
deriving from this symbol, but garden mazes in Tudor times were created
more for pleasure than for meaning. 'Treading the maze', as expelling the
Devil, was part of a three-day June fair granted by Royal charter in 1353.
Shakespeare recalls the custom—fairies and all—in 1594:

The nine men's morris is filled up with mud;
And the quaint mazes in the wanton green
For lack of tread, are undistinguishable.

[*A Midsummer Night's Dream*]

Though the mazes of Tudor houses and palaces had lost their devilish origin, a 'sacred circle' for the practice of the black arts was by no means uncommon. As early as AD 601, Pope Gregory sent a message to St Augustine:

> I have reached the conclusion that the temples of the idols in England should not on any account be destroyed. Augustine must smash the idols, but the temples themselves should be sprinkled with holy water and altars set up in them in which relics are to be enclosed. For we ought to take advantage of well-built temples by purifying them from devil-worship and dedicating them to the service of the true God. In this way, I hope the people will leave their idolatry as where of old they sacrificed cattle to devils and yet continue to frequent the places as formerly, so coming to know and revere the true God.

Far from accepting 'the true God', many Englishmen kept their temples. The mysteries, so important to man and constantly a conflict of civic and ecclesiastical argument, went underground and joined up with pre-Christian ceremony and ritual. The sacred services was held at night and often continued until dawn of the following day. (The 'fairy time' was always at night.) Sometimes in buildings, sometimes even in churches, these rituals were usually held in the open air in the woods, hills and mountains, or on the moors in their sacred circles. The old pre-Christian giant hill figures cut into the turf were used. One, Cerne (= 'stone') Giant in Dorset, is an enormous nude figure holding a club and associated with early fertility rites. May Day celebrations must have taken place near him, for there is a maypole area and a simple maze cut into the hillside close to his image. A general belief was that a hitherto barren woman, sleeping all night on his erect penis, would become fertile and able to bear children. Many of the (some six hundred) standing stones and stone circles, scattered over the British Isles—in most instances accurately calculating the movements of the sun, moon and major stars during the year—were no doubt also used for 'underground' ritual.

The supernatural was always hovering over medieval life, but heavy penalties were inflicted on those practising 'heathen' cults. Folk nevertheless continued to offer sacrifice to the spirit of a tree, stone, river or spring. The earth was always revered. The old earth-mother continually brings forth life and so, with death, man's natural instinct is that life should return again. Rituals were whispered of blood-scattering on the fields, death through suffocation of people buried alive, and communal sex. Old gods became devils, fairies, elves, witches and hob-goblins. 'Hob' goblins were another reminder of 'Robin's' power ('Hob' being a nickname for 'Robin'). Fairies appeared on Midsummer's Night, May Day and Hallow-e'en, and attended marriages and births. Everyone believed they danced and lived on hills and mounts. When a lady was brought to bed with child, the bell of the local church rang out to ask favour from the saints (the good fairies or spirits). Its tolling also controlled the time of labour and the time for rest. The same bell, suspended between heaven and earth, sounded its burial peals to ward off evil spirits (sprites) from the soul of the dead. In many of our churches the North side is supposed to belong to the Devil. A small door—the 'Devil's door'—is opened only during baptisms and communion to permit the evil spirit to escape.

If someone stole his cow, the farmer might still, however, cast a spell on him in the name of Christ—'May the cross of Christ bring it back from the East'. The Normans may have brought with them their Christian 'wise men' and astrologers, but the English still dedicated their flowers and trees . to pagan gods: dittany (an oily plant) to the Moon (worship of the moon was very important during the sixteenth century—see *A Midsummer Night's Dream*); myrtle to Venus; oak to Jupiter. The oak-tree, also sacred to the Celts often became the centre for a large fair—one was held regularly in Hainault forest in Essex. The vine was associated with blood, the palm with victory, and orange blossom with virginity. Myrtle and rosemary were for death and funerals; the yew was the tree of death and, being evergreen, was planted in the churchyard, where it was said to spread its roots to the mouth of every corpse.

Private or sacred dance led to a revival of strange 'mystical' ritual which credited a chosen person with supernatural powers. As the Christian religion was entirely male in its chosen leaders, it was sometimes a female (the earth goddess) who led the private gathering. The coven was a gathering of twelve witches (male or female) and the leader—the Devil, no doubt in imitation of Christ and the apostles—a solemn grouping. The secret rituals and meetings held irrespective of Church and civic dogma were governed by specific times in the year. A broom was used as part of the ceremonial dance:

'And I am sent with broom before, to sweep the dust behind the door'

. . . and so our pantomime witch rides on a broomstick. Medieval ceremonies of witchcraft and Satan-worship attracted many accusations, including those of cannibalism and child sacrifice. The eating of flesh was immediately associated with the power of the sacrificed entering the living. Certainly the symbol of purification and worship by fire and of fire was common; and so condemned witches preferred death by fire. The Church in France allowed witches to die by burning but in England 'heretics died at the stake, whilst those found guilty of witchcraft were strangled. The English Church distinguished between thought and practice: it did not question the existence of witchcraft (all ancient civilisations had their diviners, necromancers, soothsayers and conjurors) and accepted 'Grand masters' and the existence of faculties for practising the black arts; but, provided the practitioners did not attack Christian belief directly, the authorities preferred to argue about their own immediate problems—protestant or Catholic. It is interesting to note that witchcraft was not a capital offence in England until 1563 and that the first known record of an English witch hanged is dated 1566. Soon many were to be tried and condemned to death—were they not Satan's prime servants?

Queen Elizabeth was not alone in finding life tiresome in 1600. Politically, the noblemen had no wars, little chivalry and no future; the clergy—at war with themselves—no longer held the faith of the ordinary man; and the ordinary man had nothing to comprehend but his own poverty. The arts in society were, on the surface, purely decorative—or couched with hidden symbols and secret signs. All 'old' drama was rigorously censored and many 'new' plays were filled with horror, cynicism, nightmare and 'black' tragedy. Any popular music was suspect and dancing was the only entertainment common to all, artificial at Court and mostly clandestine in the country.

Man was, not for the first time, in confusion.

Bringing home, and dancing around the Maypole

Amorous encounters, dancing, & mystical ceremonies are associated with trees. The Oak & the Ash were particularly revered by the Celts & the Norsemen. The Worship springs from the knowledge that the tree had seen, & was to see life far beyond the life span of Man.

On the Left-Circle Dancing around a tree C15th. Below is a symbolic representation of the tree of life - a combination of South & North European belief.

JACK OF
THE GREEN
conjectural

3 HORNED MASKS

TWO FOLLOW-MY LEADER DANCES (originally pre Christi

*all based on contemporary manuscripts*

*d a group of* MUSICIANS & MUMMERS *dressed as animals*

14th

Minstrels, Mummers or Morris Dancers

Plough-Monday Celebrations—
Plough-boys dancing,
accompanied by music and
with characters dressed as a
fool and a man disguised as
Maid Marian or an old lady.
c. 1830's.

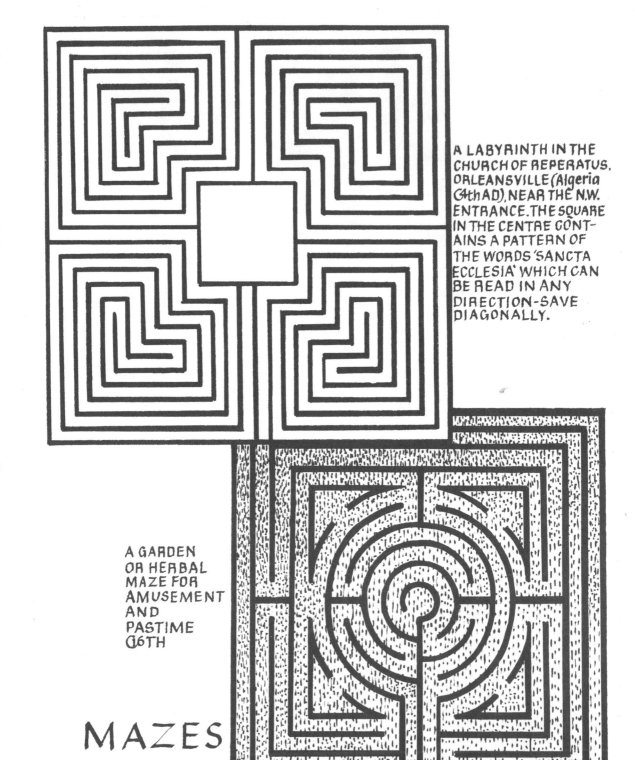

A LABYRINTH IN THE
CHURCH OF REPERATUS,
ORLEANSVILLE (Algeria
(4th AD), NEAR THE N.W.
ENTRANCE. THE SQUARE
IN THE CENTRE CONT-
AINS A PATTERN OF
THE WORDS 'SANCTA
ECCLESIA' WHICH CAN
BE READ IN ANY
DIRECTION-SAVE
DIAGONALLY.

A GARDEN
OR HERBAL
MAZE FOR
AMUSEMENT
AND
PASTIME
(16TH

MAZES

A GARDEN MAZE DESIGNED BY SERLIO

BELOW: A SHEPHERDS' RING OR
SPIRAL AT BOUGHTON GREEN
IN NORTHAMPTONSHIRE. THE
TREADING OF THE MAZE WAS
PART OF A THREE-DAY FAIR
DATING FROM THE REIGN OF
EDWARD III in 1353. THE
SPIRAL IS CUT INTO THE TURF.
IT IS INTERESTING TO NOTE
THAT AN ALMOST IDENTICAL
LABYRINTH EXISTS AT
CHARTRES CATHEDRAL (13th,
AND ANOTHER AT
LUCCA IN ITALY

MAZES

# THE GIANT OF CERNE ABBAS DORSET

some 60 feet away - a mystic area, of mounds and ditches; (possibly a site for ceremonial spiral and maypole dancing.)

80 feet

100 feet

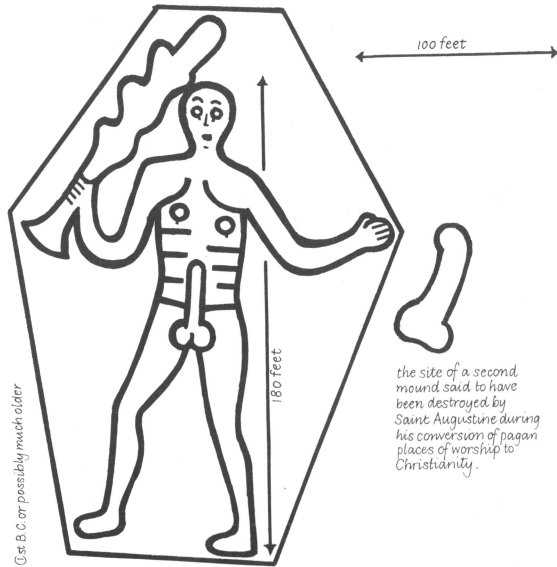

180 feet

(1st B.C. or possibly much older

the site of a second mound said to have been destroyed by Saint Augustine during his conversion of pagan places of worship to Christianity.

Cumbrian Stone Circle

Stonehenge

THE MOON · THE SYMBOL
OF THE VIRGIN

WOMEN DANCING BY THE LIGHT
OF THE FULL MOON c 1480

Conjectural Drawing of Herne the Hunter & his pack of Phantom Hounds

from a woodcut in the BM

based on Olaus Magnus 1555

Circle Dancing: above-Robin Goodfellow in the Circle: below-Elves and Horned Gods

*from the title page of the edition of 1626*

Doctor Faustus, in his magic circle conjuring the Devil

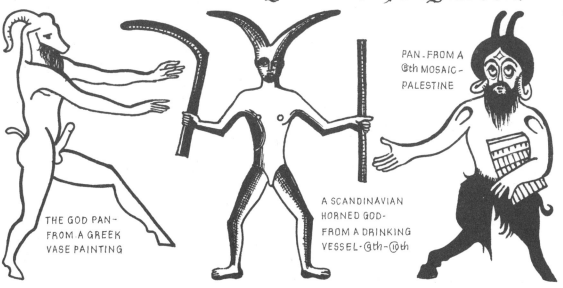

THE GOD PAN - FROM A GREEK VASE PAINTING

A SCANDINAVIAN HORNED GOD - FROM A DRINKING VESSEL · 6th - 10th

PAN - FROM A 6th MOSAIC - PALESTINE

# THE HORNED GOD CULT AND WORSHIP

Witches burnt by Fire

Fire and Light Ritual (including
tree lopping) in Epping Forest, Essex.
c. 1800's.

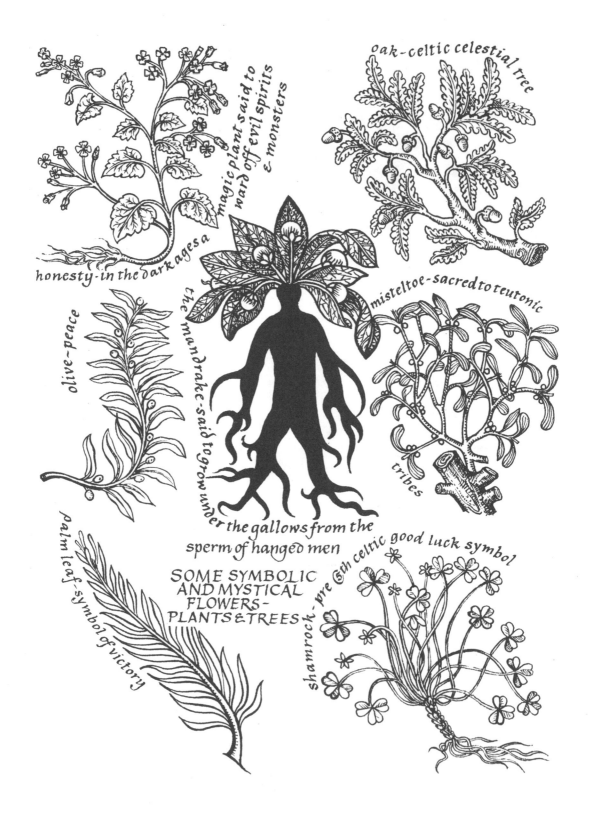

honesty·in the dark ages a

magic plant said to ward off evil spirits & monsters

oak-celtic celestial tree

olive~peace

misteltoe-sacred to teutonic tribes

the mandrake-said to grow under the gallows from the sperm of hanged men

palm leaf-symbol of victory

shamrock-pre 6th celtic good luck symbol

SOME SYMBOLIC AND MYSTICAL FLOWERS-PLANTS & TREES

# Epilogue

Degree being vizarded,
The unworthiest shows as fairly in the mask.
The heavens themselves, the planets and this centre,
Observe degree, priority and place,
Insisture, course, proportion, season, form,
Office and custom, in all line of order:
And therefore is the glorious planet Sol
In noble eminence enthroned and sphered
Amidst the other: whose med'cinable eye
Corrects the ill aspects of planets evil,
And posts like the commandment of a king,
Sans check to good and bad. But when the planets
In evil mixture to disorder wanders,
What plagues and what portents, what mutiny,
With raging of the sea, shaking of earth,
Commotion in the winds, frights, changes, horrors,
Divert and crack, rend and deracinate
The unity and married calm of states
Quite from their fixture! Oh! when degree is shaked,
Which is the ladder of all high designs,
The enterprise is sick! How could communities,
Degrees in schools and brotherhoods in cities,
Peaceful commerce from dividable shore,
The primogenity and due of birth,
Prerogative of age, crown, sceptres, laurels,
But by degree, stand in authentic place?
Take but degree away, untune that string,
And, hark, what discord follows! Each thing meets

In mere oppugnancy. The bounded waters
Should lift their bosoms higher than the shores,
And make a sop of all this solid globe;
Strength should be lord of imbecility,
And the rude son should strike his father dead;
Force should be right, or rather, right and wrong,
Between whose endless jar justice resides,
Should lose their names, and so should justice too.
Then everything includes itself in power,
Power into will, will into appetite;
And appetite, an universal wolf,
So doubly seconded with will and power,
Must make performance an universal prey,
And last eat up himself.

Shakespeare, *Troilus and Cressida*

# Postscript

Why does the world want entertainment? The question produces many answers, sometimes mystical and sacred; sometimes profane, sometimes politic (and all sometimes, because of necessity, performed 'underground'). Rich and poor alike need instruction, all need faith, and all need a therapeutic outlet from the conditions imposed upon them by their society or civilisation. Sometimes we need to entertain ourselves; sometimes to be entertained—uplifted or brought down to earth. Sometimes we need to be highly organised to a strictly formal pattern; at other times to be free from restrictions so that we can behave just as we please. The drama and paradox of life must be released in all of us when trying to solve the conflict between our spiritual aspirations and the basic animality existing deep down below the surface of human life, which often cannot find a natural outlet in the social structure we have to come to terms with. This, then, is the history of entertainment and ritual from the beginning of man's struggle for freedom from the restrictions of his own beginnings and throughout his slow development into a social being.

The basic aim of the performer, professional or amateur, is to involve a collection of people with an idea and to evolve a method of presentation or means of expression which communicates the idea to its audience. He always tries, no matter how, to move the head or the heart of his audience, stimulating the intellect and/or the emotions.

How is the idea expressed? On an elementary level, by such cartoons as we see in our evening newspapers ('Bristow' and 'Modesty Blaise'). Then comes the necessity to vivify the communication by movement and we get, on television, 'Tom and Jerry' and 'Batman'. Words are spoken and sounds of varying length make special patterns of rhythm by means of which the idea can be more fully realised. Shakespeare needs a whole consort of word and sound structures to hold and give full meaning to his themes. The

215

choice of prose, blank verse, rhymed verse, emphasises the ebb and flow of the action of the play and brings out its subtle implications. A rhymed couplet may serve to emphasise a moment of finality. Lyric verse comes close to the operatic aria, allowing the voice to rise and fall and sing with such exquisite beauty that the idea is transported into the realm of the magic and mystery of music. Viola's lyrical wooing of Olivia on behalf of Orsino in *Twelfth Night* is of this nature. The singing voice, accompanied either by the actor himself or a group of musicians, adds something to the action or helps to change the mood of a scene. Musicians, in their own right, made music to enrich in a way which could not be done with speech. Music supports, and, in many instances, has a much stronger dramatic value than words, as in the effect of 'Let there be still music until she dies'. The sounds of battle with trumpets and drums or the sound of a striking clock, thunder, gunfire, or the sound of birds: all contribute to the idea of entertainment.

The performer, in early civilisations, had to rely on movement, gesture, and dance. The spoken word developed well after man's first instinct to communicate through gesture or 'emotive sounds' (just as babies make noises from birth, but for many months it is their gesture patterns and facial expressions that give us the most important clues as to what they are thinking or wanting). In the same way the actor had to develop a series of actions to further the action and express his character. He had to indicate by carefully selected movements where he was, whither he was going and, by gesture and facial expression, his emotion at the time. Later he added pieces of scenery or used light to indicate place or time. In the Greek theatre the movement of the sun itself timed the action, as during the days of the great dramatic festivals in honour of Dionysus when the plays started with the rising of the sun and ended with its setting. With scenery also came costume, dressing up to create magic in a ritual, or wearing fancy-dress to impersonate a character. Adding simple properties and furniture to the scenery finally helped convey the world in which he was placed.

Where did he set up his 'world'? Often claiming divine guidance, he in fact chose anywhere with good sight-lines for his audience. Dramatic communication did not start in a building, but in a place open to the elements, which often became a sacred area or even the temple itself. Later theatres were specially designed for the professional. In Greece these were usually on a steep hillside (Persepolis) or in a wood (Epidaurus). The Romans built huge 'stages' on the sea or on artificial lakes *(Naumachiae)* for the presentation of mock sea battles. Throughout his history the performer has used any street corner, any hearth, any 'open place'.

But besides needing an audience, *he needed to eat.* So he was dependent on the society in which he lived, its moral codes, its ethics and its philosophy, and patronage. He was governed by, or rebelled against, the religious dictates of the clerics and the authority of kings. He was bound by heritage, place of birth, the seasons and by the extent of his own personal discoveries. But all performers had a common aim—to use their talents to reveal to man what *they* understood about the life they were given through story, sounds, movements and visual display.

The organisation of group performing evolved from the celebration of some 'rite', later to become a permanent celebration in the civilisation's calendar, a custom or practice to be regularly observed and to be respected. One such ritual can be seen in cave paintings: in these early days of man's history the hunter would draw or paint on the walls of his cave pictures of the animals he had killed so that his children knew what they looked like. By dressing up a friend in the skin of the animal, he could act out in pantomime the killing of the beast which had provided food, clothing and bone for tools to sustain his family or his tribe. Before every hunt he repeated the pantomime and it finally became a ritual. The ritual may eventually have become an act of superstition but the pantomime may equally well have been carried into the hunt itself and therefore have been an essential dress-rehearsal. (Today's Eskimo still dresses in a sealskin to track down the seal, moving with floppy movements and making the noise of the seal during his progress over the ice.)

Other group rituals were in the form of symbolic movement, particularly those representing sun and moon worship. These were solemn observances, essential to heart and head and to life itself. Early civilisation had little time for comedy and laughter. Life was hard. Life had to be taken seriously and respected. It was centred on a series of acts of worship, a recognition on the part of man of some higher unseen power controlling his destiny, requiring obedience. Although the ritual was symbolic, the masks, make-up and costume he used were at times highly naturalistic, using colour, texture, shape and ornament to tell his audience or communicants the story and identity of the reverence.

Linked with solemn observance and belief in the unknown was the natural element of basic man-fear, expressed in superstition and 'acts' to ward off ill omens. Many such primitive acts we still observe today. We still toss salt over our shoulders, we still throw rice over the bride and bridegroom, we still touch wood. We still read what the stars have to say about us in the evening newspaper and many of us wear a talisman about our necks. And—whether we admit it or not—we still like dressing up to pretend to be, often, what we are not! Imagination occupies a large part of our thinking moments, though we mostly show it more openly in childhood. My god-daughter, for her list of Christmas presents, wrote out the following in this order: a bride's dress; a queen's dress; a witch's dress; a pretty fairy; and a crown. She is seven and loves making up her face. In school or at church she is quiet and observant, treating her studies and life with deep respect . . . but I shall remember her as an elegant bride, wearing her royal crown and dress, or suddenly descending on us with devilish laughter as a witch.

Ritual—then and now—takes many forms. It can be a solemn worship of the gods, with the performer dressed as the god or deity himself, thereby creating an act of transfiguration—the god taking possession and he, the actor, becoming god. Or it can be a method of teaching, giving imposed instructions or a series of questions, to control thought or to free it—'The bogey man will catch you if you don't watch out!'. A ritual can be created by the State, or the elders of a community, to teach and make clear a warning to the observers to be always obedient and to observe the law! Its power is great and as Tolstoy said, 'the theatre is the strongest pulpit for the modern man'.

But, through time and wisdom, every good civilisation knew that it was necessary for man to laugh, to play games and simply to enjoy himself without fear of guilt or recrimination—to allow for the spontaneous moment of pleasure without searching for reason or purpose. Entertainers with whatever talent they possessed (or believed in) did 'their own thing', singing, dancing, telling stories, dressing up, making simple instruments to blow, pluck or bang; and made 'fools' of themselves by acting and playing 'the Ass'.

Many went their own way and founded the profession of theatre and entertainment. Some 'stars'—though they are a minority—exaggerate their needs and dress, and some become part of the Establishment, but many young actors have again taken to the streets or pubs, presenting their own precious values of life, and are returning once again to the open air—the sun, the stars, the moon and the sky . . . and to the wind and the rain.

Theatre did not arise under a fine custom-built temple or amphitheatre of socially-orientated luxury. It sprang from the very essence of life itself, to glorify and to retell the story of Man, understanding the mysteries of his heritage, his fears, and his pride, with joy and anger. In the theatre this understanding is passed on to, and shared by, his fellow man. Priests, kings, sages, mystics, scholars, actors, pantomimists, singers, dancers, acrobats, tumblers, funnymen, 'strip' and 'drag' artistes, and musicians, together with after-dinner speakers, all have their parts to play in the history of entertainment and ritual.

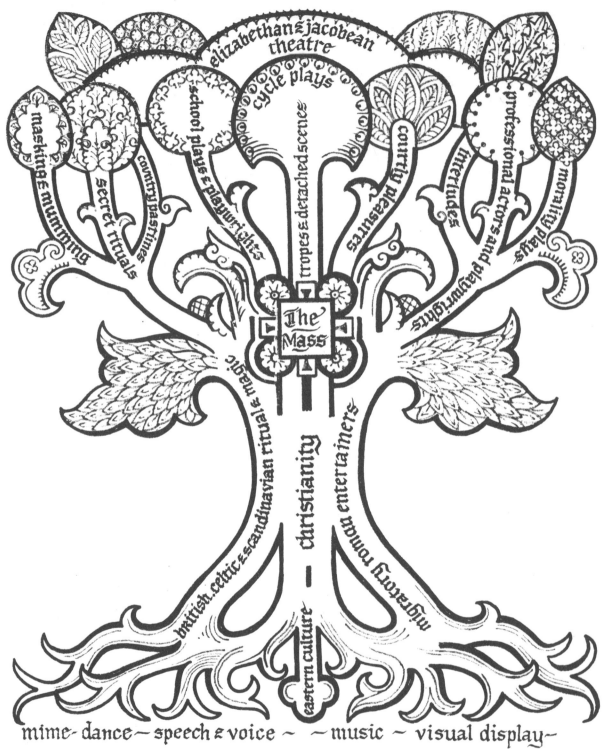

The Tree of Early English Ritual and Entertainments

# Index